BUSINESS BY DESIGN

Grammar Factory Publishing
MacMillan Company Limited
25 Telegram Mews, 39th Floor, Suite 3906
Toronto, Ontario, Canada
M5V 3Z1

www.grammarfactory.com

Green, Chris, 1969–
Business by Design: Take Your Business from Chaos and Overwhelm to Scalable and Rewarding / Chris Green.

Paperback ISBN 978-1-998756-05-6
eBook ISBN 978-1-998756-06-3

    1. BUS025000 BUSINESS & ECONOMICS / Entrepreneurship. 2. BUS060000 BUSINESS & ECONOMICS / Small Business. 3. BUS106000 BUSINESS & ECONOMICS / Mentoring & Coaching.

Production Credits
Cover design by Designerbility
Interior layout design by Dania Zafar
Book production and editorial services by Grammar Factory Publishing

Grammar Factory's Carbon Neutral Publishing Commitment
Grammar Factory Publishing is proud to be neutralizing the carbon footprint of all printed copies of its authors' books printed by or ordered directly through Grammar Factory or its affiliated companies through the purchase of Gold Standard-Certified International Offsets.

Disclaimer
The material in this publication is of the nature of general comment only and does not represent professional advice. It is not intended to provide specific guidance for particular circumstances, and it should not be relied on as the basis for any decision to take action or not take action on any matter which it covers. Readers should obtain professional advice where appropriate, before making any such decision. To the maximum extent permitted by law, the author and publisher disclaim all responsibility and liability to any person, arising directly or indirectly from any person taking or not taking action based on the information in this publication.

BUSINESS BY DESIGN

Take Your Business from Chaos and Overwhelm to Scalable and Rewarding

CHRIS GREEN

GRAMMAR FACTORY
— EST<u>D</u> 2013 —

Contents

About the Author

Chris Green is an entrepreneurial strategist, author, mentor and facilitator, and works across a broad range of industries.

Chris started his practice in 2001 in Wangaratta, Victoria. He has more than twenty years' experience in management consulting, supporting entrepreneurial SME owners to grow their businesses and realise their leadership potential.

Chris has worked with and supported some of regional Australia's most successful family-based businesses. He is always looking to represent the needs of the business in partnership with the entrepreneur to achieve strong outcomes and outstanding business results.

Having owned and operated a number of regional businesses, Chris has great empathy and understanding of the challenges facing SME owners. Noted for thinking outside the box, his creativity and passion shine through and set him apart.

A keen member of his community, Chris believes in giving back. Chris has sat on many community boards and completed a combined thirteen years as president of two cricket clubs. He is a life member of the Wangaratta Magpies Cricket Club.

Chris has an MBA (Strategic Management) from Charles Sturt University, an advanced diploma in Hospitality Management, a qualification as a Registrar of the Magistrates Court of Victoria, and is a qualified Chef.

A Business by Design

The Journey

Nathan Talbot[1] had just turned forty-four. He saw himself as a typical suburban Australian man. He had been married for almost twenty years, his wife had a career of her own and they had two kids – Emily, twelve, and Mark, eight. A lot of people would be envious of the life Nathan had created for himself. He had a lot of the things that people believe represent success – nice house, two cars and a boat to take the kids fishing on weekends.

Nathan owned a business he was immensely proud of, having created it and built it up from scratch. On the surface, the business was extremely successful; and had grown dramatically in its first few years. Nathan was far from risk averse. This was clearly demonstrated by the fact he had left a good paying job in his

---

1 Nathan Talbot is not a real person, but he could be – his story is all too common.

early thirties to bravely strike out on his own, to be his own boss and to access the type of freedom and lifestyle not possible as an employee in a nine to five job.

It had taken a little while for the business to get off the ground, but before long, Nathan had a few customers who loved his products, loved his service and loved him. He found himself to be particularly creative at this time, continually taking inspiration and suggestions for improvement from his customers. He was able to leverage these ideas into his and meet his customers' every demand. At this point he wasn't making any money, but he was learning a lot and he found the interaction with his customers and their delight in his products particularly satisfying.

During these embryonic stages of the business, Nathan worked hard and spent long hours in the office. He didn't see a lot of his family; however, they fully understood the sacrifices Nathan had to make to get their business off the ground. They were incredibly supportive because they knew that down the track, when the business became established, there would be lots of time to come together as a family and enjoy the fruits of Nathan's labour.

It didn't take long for word to spread about Nathan and his products and service. More and more customers came and the business grew rapidly. Growth happened because the business was agile and able to customise its products and services to individual demands. This was something the big boys couldn't do, and something Nathan's customers valued. Nathan continued to work hard; however, the creative glow that had sustained him in those first few months was starting to fade. He was not feeling so creative now. He seemed to be working longer and longer hours, but that was okay, because he knew that when his business reached a critical size, he could take a step back and do the things that he wanted to do. The sacrifice would be worth it.

It's likely that many of you can see some of Nathan's story in your own. A highly creative, inspired beginning, hard work and long hours to get lift-off, then the thrill of customers buying your product – which led you to put in longer and longer hours.

Nathan's business continued to grow on the back of its ability to out-do the big boys by meeting and often exceeding customer demands. After all, the customer was always right. But while the business was extremely busy and had plenty of customers, Nathan was now exhausted and overwhelmed. And the business wasn't just busy – it was chaotic. Nathan had been running fast for a long time and had run out of steam. Despite this, he soldiered on. The business had become known for its customisation and responsiveness, and Nathan was reluctant to push back on customer demands. He didn't want his customers to go elsewhere. Things got so bad he dreaded going to work. He wasn't sleeping and spent a lot of the night tossing and turning, while mentally reliving the day or working through problems likely to come up the next day.

> *No matter how hard you work, the business problems just seem to compound!*

In Nathan's case, the chaos of the day to day meant that products started being delivered late, mistakes were being made and the customers were not loving him like they used to. Everything had begun to feel out of control.

His staff, who had traditionally been great employees – highly engaged and good problem solvers – were now getting disgruntled. They were sick of the chaos, the daily battles, and having to respond reactively to issues that may not have arisen had the business been better organised.

The situation at home was not much better. Nathan's wife was now justifiably fed up with not seeing her husband and having to parent alone. Nathan had missed too many special occasions, such as his kids' sporting events and ballet recitals. These were things he used to love and part of the reason he started the business in the first place. He thought being his own boss would give him more time to spend with his kids. Nathan felt under siege from all angles, and it had been like this for a long time. The fishing boat, needless to say, had not been out in months.

Ten years after he started the business, Nathan, who had been so full of inspiration and enthusiasm, was now beat. He had tried a lot of different ways to bring sanity to his business and his life, but every time he bounced back, rebooted and remodelled, the business would eventually begin experiencing the same problems and the porpoising cycle would begin again.

You may be reading this book because you are experiencing problems running your SME. Like Nathan, you have probably tried lots of different strategies to turn your business around, but end up just tinkering around the edges and not effecting any real change. I suspect there will be many elements of Nathan's story to which you relate.

> ## *Nathan is trapped below the entrepreneurial ceiling!*

But what is the entrepreneurial ceiling?

Do you remember the film *Titanic*, and the scene in which Leonardo DiCaprio's character, Jack, is trapped in a cabin below deck that is rapidly filling with water? The water dramatically rushes into the cabin as the ship begins to sink, but there are still small pockets of air under the ceiling. Jack desperately pushes his face against the ceiling to take a breath in a pocket of air while frantically trying to think of a way out. This is what life under the entrepreneurial ceiling can feel like. There will be times when your day is consumed by firefighting one issue after another.

You become highly reactive to customers, staff and suppliers. There are never enough hours in the day, or days in the week. It's endless, it's relentless and it's not what you envisaged when you created or purchased your business.

The great news is that you can break through the entrepreneurial ceiling to a business that provides freedom, satisfaction and even joy. A business that provides a great lifestyle for you and your family. A business that is scalable and rewarding. Millions of businesses have trod this path before you.

But while this journey is simple, it is not easy. It will require you to let go and face your fears. It is these fears that have you photocopying the same day repeatedly and keeping you and your business stuck. You must let go of the fear of the unknown and embrace uncertainty. Commit to being different, to doing things differently, and to operating in a way that will feel unfamiliar to you.

Adopting a breakthrough mindset will allow you to face challenges from a different perspective. A new, disciplined approach will form the foundations for your business.

Through this book I will show you how you can create an aspirational path so compelling that it will sustain the journey, provide a new perspective when things are tough and inspire others to follow.

You will learn the power of creating a winning team. A team of skilled individuals with the processes and capacity to play their role. With the ability to proactively drive the customer experience and product outcomes and connect with each other in a way that leads to sustainable success.

You will learn how to remove yourself as the bottleneck – the single point of failure – and leverage your knowledge into business systems that will enable others to do what you once did.

Willpower alone will not get you there. You must redesign your environment so that no matter how tempting it is to go back to the old ways, the organisational environment, its business systems and its people make it virtually impossible.

My wish for you is that you recapture the feeling you had when you first commenced your business journey. That raw enthusiasm, the exhilaration of the first sale, the adulation of your customers. Many of you may not have felt this for years. It's time to get to work.

As a regional management consultant who has mentored and coached entrepreneurs and business owners like you for over twenty years and owned and run my own small business … I get it, and I have empathy for your plight. The journey to create a business by design that serves you, your family and your lifestyle can be a long and arduous one. It is an emotional journey with many pitfalls and stumbles, and the odd trip. It is both exhilarating and exasperating. While you can see the peak, you may find yourself trapped beneath an imaginary ceiling – the entrepreneurial ceiling – unable to go forward, unable to go back.

Everything contained in this book is told through the lens of personal experience. Having owned and operated my own SME, as well as mentored hundreds of other family-based businesses, I get it. I have lived it, I feel it. I understand where you're at and the challenges you face. I understand how running a business is not a nine to five job but, rather, it is reflective of who you are and what you value.

I have great empathy and admiration for you, the brave souls who have backed yourselves and ventured out to forge your own path. This book is the culmination of the journeys of many others – journeys I have had a ringside seat to. The journeys of business owners just like you, who have gone from chaos and overwhelm to freedom and reward. Owners who have put in place the building blocks that have ultimately led to their business by design.

Creating a business by design is not for the faint hearted. But those who have achieved breakthrough, and there are plenty, will tell you they would not swap their journey for the world. They have created a wonderful business that serves them, their families and their people.

A purposeful SME business is a richly rewarding and creative endeavour. A vehicle that enables you to showcase your passion and your skill in the day to day, it provides a lifestyle that serves you and your family. It should not be like a job, but more like a calling that provides you with the creative freedom to choose. Choose work you love, the way you like. If this is what you seek, then follow me and let the transformation begin.

1

Commit to Doing Differently

What got you here won't get you there

It was half past six on a frosty winter morning when Craig's alarm set off the annoying series of high-pitched screeches and beeps designed to startle him out of deep sleep and into the new day.

As Craig opened his eyes and gradually got his bearings, a sense of dread overtook him – as it did most days. Craig had always dreamed of owning and running his own business, and there had been a time that the alarm would signal the start of an exciting new day. But it didn't feel like that these days, and every bone in his body wanted to pull the covers over his head and hope the world would go away. Instead, he slowly and reluctantly pulled himself out of bed and headed for the shower.

Craig found taking a shower meditative, and often drifted away in thought. On this morning, as he had on many other mornings, he found himself wondering, 'How did it come to this?' He had started his business with the dream of being his own boss. To create wealth for himself and his family. To provide free time and a lifestyle that let him choose what he did and when he did it. No boss telling him what to do and no nine to five clock-watching; instead, the thrill of being able to do it on *his* terms.

The first few years of his cabinet making business had been exhilarating and intense. Craig loved every second of it. He worked at his business from home and, after a few false starts, the customers began to appear. One by one they came, with requests to do this and can you do that. Craig was highly creative in meeting his customers' demands, and they loved it. They loved him.

He began to hire staff to service the demand as he moved into a high growth phase, and more and more customers came. Craig's point of difference, as he saw it, was his ability to meet customer demands and customise his services to whatever his customers needed. His bigger, less agile competitors could not do this and made the customers conform to a standard range, standard colours, standard products and standard service. Clearly, these competitors didn't 'get' what the customers needed.

Although the business was not making much money, if any, at this stage, more and more customers came and Craig continued to deploy what he saw as his competitive advantage by reacting to their needs. He got his customers and they got him. His business was growing fast, and he was thrilled with the success.

But the relentless growth was exhausting. Craig had hired more and more people to keep up with demand, and now he was spending a lot of his time managing the people and the clients. There never seemed to be enough time in the day.

The business had become so successful it had outgrown its premises and now needed new, bigger, more expensive facilities. Craig's range of offerings had also increased to meet the endless wish lists of customers that, of course, Craig catered for. He needed so much inventory that he now had to have an overdraft facility to meet the demand. And some customers had become a bit slack in paying their bills, so Craig hired a full-time book keeper to chase the debts and manage the cash.

The challenge was that the whole business relied on Craig and his operational knowledge to function. After all, the business had got to this point based on his skill and know-how. It was true that no one could do it as well as Craig. But by the time he showed other people what to do, he might as well have done it himself – so he did.

As Craig worked longer and longer hours to try to get through the endless to-do list, his energy levels dropped, his health suffered and his family hardly saw him. Craig had started a business for lifestyle, freedom of choice and wealth creation. None of these things had eventuated. He was trapped in an endless cycle and had no clue how he was going to get out of it. The business was in a state of chaos, and he was overwhelmed. It was relentless and suffocating at the same time.

This is what life under the entrepreneurial ceiling feels like. Trapped in the overwhelming and chaotic day to day, Craig put one foot in front of the other and soldiered on.

This pattern of destructive growth is repeated in entrepreneurial businesses everywhere.

When you start or take over your business, you are naturally optimistic for the future and brimming with enthusiasm. You feel highly creative and have so many ideas you literally ping around the room.

You built the business and overcame obstacles with sheer will-power and determination, so when faced with adversity you find a way to scale the wall, dig under it, go around it or bust through it. You have no notion of nine to five. An intoxicating blend of passion, inspiration, ambition and curiosity comes together in a potent cocktail that enables your creative juices to flow.

I have worked with entrepreneurs – people like you – for a long time, and have come to recognise very distinct patterns in the journey. Although your products differ, your leadership styles differ and your businesses differ, there is a similarity, consistency and pattern to the journey you are all on.

While you believe your path is unique and yours alone to tread, this is simply not true. Your path has been walked many millions of times before. It is not so much a path as it is a rock climb. Inch by inch, handhold by handhold, foothold by foothold, you scale the sheer cliff face. Progress is slow. Sometimes you fall. Sometimes you take risks that skirt the edge of human capability, and other times you're more conservative. The rewards when you reach the pinnacle are often breathtaking. An extraordinary sense of accomplishment. Spectacular vistas. Sheer exhaustion. All these feelings, emotions and sensory delights combine to say you have made it. You have challenged every fibre of your being and made it. Then it's on to the next challenge.

While the journey of owning and operating your own enterprise is no less challenging than scaling a sheer rock face, my experience has been that, unlike scaling a cliff, your path to success is rarely clear. Most entrepreneurs don't really know where the finishing line is, what it looks like or how they are going to get there. You wake up every morning with a passion to do better, be better, become better. But the reality is, unless you do something substantially different on that brand-new day, you are likely to get results similar to the days before.

For many of you, the daily grind is an endless battle through the weeds that forces you to be highly reactive to the stuff that relentlessly comes at you. The reality is that, unless you truly address the root cause of the problem that is keeping you stuck, you will have to get out your metaphorical machete and furiously hack at the weeds day after day after day. You will be assaulted by an endless stream of people issues, supply issues, quality issues and customer issues.

You are so busy putting out fires that you rarely, if ever, take the time to consider what success does and should look like. On the very odd occasion you have allocated time to work *on* the business, not *in* it, you find yourself playing catch up with email and doing draining admin tasks that could be done faster and better by someone else.

When your very long day, longer than any of your employees, is finally done, your to-do list sits untouched. You go home, fall in an exhausted heap and drift off to sleep on the couch in front of the television. Then you do it all again tomorrow.

Let's face it, it's not all bad. There are brief moments when you're engulfed by a euphoric high. When you pull off something so spectacular and satisfying that you want to yell and leap in the air. A sale you didn't think you could make. The warm flood of emotion as a happy customer waxes lyrical about your product or service. On these rare occasions, a rush of adrenaline hits like a freight train and, for a second, the joy of winning washes over you and creates a sense of extraordinary validation for all the hard times and the times when you and others doubted your ability to succeed. It is at these times that you remember why you got into business in the first place. These moments are intoxicating and flood the brain with feel-good chemicals. But without addressing the problems in your business, these moments become just a fleeting, false dawn. They're rare, but we chase them nonetheless.

The entrepreneurial journey is punctuated by the highest of highs and the lowest of lows. The fortunes of the business can wildly fluctuate based on the energy of you, the entrepreneur. The entrepreneur who is the source of all knowledge and the technical guru. When your energy is up, the business goes up. Business development activity brings in a stream of new work. People are inspired and passionate. The energy is infectious and the whole place is buzzing.

When your energy goes down, business fortunes often go with you. Nothing seems to go right. Everyone is overwhelmed, and most of all you – the business owner. Customers are dissatisfied, quality is an issue, supply chain is lumpy and systems are falling down everywhere. You're in the weeds and every day feels like a fire fight. The business is at capacity, you are overwhelmed and chaos is everywhere. There is no sense of control, no respite from the pressure.

This cycle, in which the business fortunes mirror your entrepreneurial energy, is what I call porpoising. It reflects the up and down movement a porpoise's tail makes as it propels through the water. The shape of the movement mimics how you feel. A business whose performance cycles up and down reflects the energy levels of the business owner. You.

The point where demand outstrips supply is the point where you hit the entrepreneurial ceiling. Output builds to a crescendo on the back of great energy and solid business wins that relied on the technical knowledge and business endeavours of you, the business owner. Unfortunately, the business game that attempts to match supply with demand rarely, and then only for the briefest of times, achieves balance.

At this stage of the cycle, demand will reach a tipping point and outstrip what you can supply. Your physical, mental and emotional capacity, which has been red-lining for so long, will finally collapse and the wave will crash over you. Overwhelm will engulf you. The business, that relies so heavily on you, will not have the resource it needs to keep the momentum going. Your time will be so limited that decision making will slow, the technical work that relies on your expertise will stagnate and the sense of being out of control will lead to anxiety. You may push back by working longer hours but, inevitably, this strategy will fail to be effective. You're out of options. The cycle has begun.

You have hit the entrepreneurial ceiling!

The Entrepreneurial Ladder

Having worked with entrepreneurial businesses and mentored their owners for a long time, I have come to recognise six distinct levels in the journey from start-up to scalable. Each level has its unique challenges and circumstances, as shown in Figure 1.

	LIFECYCLE	FOCUS	STATE
	Scalable	Visionary	Rewarding
	Consistent	Systems-Driven	Sustainable
Break-through	Transitional	Leveraged	Developmental
Ceiling	Capacity	Chaotic	Overwhelmed
	High-Growth	Customer Driven	Reactive
	Start-Up	Creative	Uncommercial

Figure 1: The entrepreneurial ladder

Start-up

Start-up, whether it be a brand-new business you designed or a renovator's delight business you have bought and are remodelling, is generally the stage where you're most creative. The reality is that you're rarely commercial at this point, as you lack the reputational resources and industry positioning to command sustainable commercial rates. So, you take what you can get. At the start-up phase, you will feel nervous, anxious, excited and scared. Often you have a back-up plan, but not always. The nature of the entrepreneur is that you are brave and bold, and back yourself. At this stage you will probably feel like an imposter fumbling around in the dark, but this will be more than offset through your creativity, inspiration and hope.

High growth

The high growth phase is incredibly exciting. Customers want your product, and these early adopters are deeply involved in helping you make your product better. You want to please, so you become highly reactive to their needs, suggestions and desires. No Henry Ford's 'one colour, take it or leave it' here. At this stage the customers can have any colour Ford they want. You have achieved lift-off and it is exhilarating. There's a mixture of disbelief that your business is firing, and pumping adrenaline as the day to day suddenly starts to fill and customers keep coming. You are waiting for the work to dry up at any second, but it doesn't. The odd lull in customers creates minor ripples of panic, but faith is soon restored as business picks up. It will feel like you're making real money, but unfortunately this can be an illusion. Cash is tied up in accounts payable, and inventory seems to fly out the door as quickly as it comes in. Nonetheless, your business now feels real and you're on your way.

Capacity

The next stage of the entrepreneurial journey is capacity. As the name suggests, this is the rung on the entrepreneurial ladder where most SME owners find themselves. It's the stage where demand outstrips supply. Where you're busy being busy and there is an overdependence on you, the entrepreneur. In your mind, you have never really taken, or even had, the time to build business systems and work on the business.

This stage is chaotic, frenetically paced, with you as the source of all knowledge. You're too busy to lead, but too busy to consider a different way. This is the stage below the entrepreneurial ceiling. I have watched business owners porpoise below the entrepreneurial ceiling for years. Never breaking through, repeating the same pattern day in and day out, desperately hoping for a different result that never comes. The entrepreneurial ceiling is an imaginary ceiling that, for many, forms an impenetrable barrier that blocks the path to success and sentences you to a business characterised by chaos and overwhelm.

It's an endless struggle and an emotional roller coaster. You're porpoising personally and professionally. Your business is stuck below the ceiling, in danger of never achieving breakthrough, and condemned to a future predicated by your energy levels and the constant struggle to try to balance supply and demand.

If you continue to do what you have done, you will continue to get what you have got. The irony is that the high demand for your business is what made it successful, but now that demand is causing so much grief. Be careful what you wish for. Caught between a rock and a hard place, you can't turn the demand tap off because if you do, cashflow will be affected and you will not be able to pay the mounting bills. But the status quo is no fun. This rung of the entrepreneurial ladder can feel suffocating, stressful and overwhelming. The day to day can become a grind and an endless procession of problems. You're up to pussy's bow in other people's problems, without making a lot of progress. It's exhausting.

> *The paradox of the entrepreneur is that what got you to today will not get you to tomorrow.*

Transitional

The levels beyond the entrepreneurial ceiling are rich with opportunity. The path here is enabled by the transition of the knowledge in your head to capable people who are guided by robust business systems. Freedom and choice are enabled by leveraging what you know, developing systems and gathering people around you who, operationally, make it happen. It's a transitional space, almost like a twilight zone, that may take a few years to work through. But once breakthrough is achieved, it provides the foundation for a business by your design highlighted by work you love that plays to your strengths, your purpose and your passion. More of what you like and less of what you don't; freedom to choose what you do, when you do it and how you do it.

This phase will take time and there may be points when you doubt the path you are on. It is a different way to do business, and letting go of doing key tasks and enabling others to do them can be challenging. This is a period of personal accountability, when delegation, not abdication, must be your leadership style. At times you will glimpse the freedom and choice that a business above the entrepreneurial ceiling offers, but at other times you will feel lost, out of control and frustrated. It is a rung that requires self-discipline, an aspirational objective and, more often than you would like, nerves of steel. You must get comfortable being uncomfortable to stay the path and transform your business.

Consistent

The fifth phase is where, for the first time, you start to see results. You know the feeling. It's like going on a diet and starting to feel fabulous, but nobody notices. Until a point in the future when, if you stay the path, suddenly everybody notices. Months or years of hard work are required to become an overnight success. You, your business systems and your capable people have been developed bit by bit, which has created a utopia where quality is constant, the business rules are well known and the work is executed consistently. Everything is under control. It is like a calm has swept over the business. At this point, you have one eye on the day to day and one eye on your aspirations for the future. The frenetic chaos you once knew under the entrepreneurial ceiling is no more. The business is sustainable.

The day to day now becomes enjoyable and you start to recapture some of the creative spark that inspired you to start the business. You have balance in your life, and everything feels lighter, more in control, happier. No longer is your day consumed by firefighting an endless stream of problems. Don't get me wrong, you will still have difficult moments, but they will be less intense and less frequent. You are scaling the entrepreneurial ladder.

Scalable

The final stage is what I call scalable. Some have called this stage sale-ready, while other more textbook-types might call it mature. To me the ability to scale a business and replicate it, or build it into a significant family-corporate enterprise, is a powerful position to be in and provides genuine possibilities and a reason to be optimistic. It is a time of choice, of entre-preneurial freedom, of opportunity. With you as the visionary, this stage gives you options. Options to do more, options to do less, options to choose.

Now that you are somewhat free of the daily operational grind, you have clean air in which to think, to dream and to ponder. Time to consider and seek new opportunities, time to leverage all your hard work and reap the rewards of your endeavours. You will have rediscovered your inner creative and, unlike the start-up phase, you will now have the time and resources to feed it properly. This is why you have undertaken this transformational journey. It will feel worth it, it will feel rewarding. You have scaled the peak. You have stored a bank of knowledge and walked a journey that many have been unable to execute.

The reality, however, is that many of you will not break through the entrepreneurial ceiling. Your hand will be cuffed to a busi-ness where overwhelm is normal and your fight, flight or freeze mechanism is constantly activated. A world where your business and personal fortunes fluctuate according to your energy as you porpoise up and down. You alternate between total exhaustion and running on fumes, and euphoric highs when you smash a home run, win a big project or receive significant recognition for your work. It's draining!

> *You will be condemned to a business life below the entrepreneurial ceiling unless you can truly change the way you do business and how you operate.*

Change starts now!

While life under the entrepreneurial ceiling is not much fun, it is the way many entrepreneurs continue to operate. So, what's truly stopping you from changing your reality?

Many entrepreneurs contact me looking for the secret sauce. That magical elixir that will remarkably and instantly transform their business so they can find balance and have the life they desire. Given that so many others have done it, surely it can't be that hard?

The good news is that this is a well-worn path and, in the pages ahead, I will outline how to tread that path. The bad news is that there is no secret sauce. It will take time, dedication and resilience. You will be challenged. There will be times when you doubt yourself and what you are doing. There will be times when it feels too hard.

This path is all about leveraging your knowledge; it's about identifying why you do what you do and what will take the business
to the next level, and truly getting to the essence of what made
the business successful in the first place. Once understood, it is
a matter of transferring that knowledge and strategic intent into
the people, business structure and processes. Sounds simple,
but it's not easy.

The business systems and processes will not be the only thing
that shifts on this transformational journey. The biggest shift
will be in you. This is a very personal transformation, which will
see you, the business owner, transition from overwhelmed and
despairing to inspired and rewarded. Living your best life, a life
by your design, a balanced life with options and choices.

There is great news for those who commit to this new path. Today,
in my view, is a great time in history to be engaged in an entrepreneurial pursuit.

*There has never been a better time in history to
make the shift and transform your business.*

Large corporate players who represent the biggest brands in the
world have successfully executed industry-defining displacement strategies. Mega companies like Apple have incredible

industry power and influence and have shifted and invented entire markets. It's easy to forget that companies like Apple, Google and Amazon all started, relatively recently, as small companies with big ideas. Guys and girls in the garage who, although small, thought big.

'That's all well and good,' I hear you say, 'but unicorns that have managed to scale to this size are rare. What about the millions of businesses like mine that, try as we may, are never likely to make such a leap or anything like it? How does citing Google, Apple and Amazon translate for me in my business, which operates in much smaller micro markets?' Great question!

While I don't believe you will or may even *want* to scale to the dizzy heights of these businesses, my view is that current conditions make transition through the entrepreneurial ceiling easier than ever before. The resources to make it happen are much more accessible and the diversity of channels to market have changed the game. And it's not just my view; there is plenty of evidence to back this up.

> *Small businesses that act like big businesses invariably become big businesses.*

Many of my entrepreneurial clients have operated in predominantly regional markets. This often means there are significantly fewer buyers than in larger markets. Fewer buyers generally means it's harder to focus on niche specialisation which, in part, drives the ability to achieve a price premium. But there are now readily available, cheap, game-changing technological applications that are providing new opportunities and levelling the playing field, making geography less relevant.

A regional market is a micro-environment where many of the industry conditions and buyer tendencies are well understood. Because they're in plain sight, it's easier to target specific buyers. The downside, as highlighted in Marc Dollinger's book, *Entrepreneurship*, and explained through his six resources model, is that if you get it wrong in a small market, your reputational resources (the hardest to acquire and sustain), will limit your market penetration. In a small market, word travels fast. Nonetheless, it is an ideal environment to explore and execute a strategic displacement game plan.

Strategic displacement is the ability to change the rules of competition, which creates a strategy that aligns the market and offering in your favour. It moves the boundaries in which you compete, enabling you to penetrate new markets and compete with limited resources.

Entrepreneurial SMEs have advantages over larger companies

and there has never been a better time to exploit these. Technology has never been cheaper, more available and more effective than it is now. The introduction of integrated software applications gives entrepreneurial businesses the ability to access data and organise themselves to be more efficient than ever before. The rise of the subscription model enabled by cloud computing means you no longer have to buy expensive servers and software programs that require continual and expensive updates. You don't need $150,000 servers or the trouble of maintaining them. Now you have the computing power at your fingertips without the financial burden and upfront cost of ownership. Game on!

In 2012, my business was purchased by a large national accounting firm with global reach and more than 200 offices across Australia. I introduced management consulting as a division of the organisation, and remember having a conversation with the partnership group and debating the merits of a $250,000 investment in a software program. This program would record client interaction, time-track and report on efficiencies, but I was taken aback by the prohibitive cost.

Fast-forward to 2018, when I went back out on my own and specialising in entrepreneurial strategy and management consulting. I was able to cobble together a financial package that was intuitive, cloud-based and easy to use. I had an integrated application that invoiced, tracked my time and reported on my efficiency, as well as a third program that operated as a coaching repository and client portal. All this for about $120 worth of sub-scriptions per month. Things had moved very quickly in those six years and the entrepreneurial SME was the big winner. The rental model of subscription and cloud-based applications has changed the game.

The COVID crisis has again accelerated Moore's law, which says that computing power will double approximately every two years. To date, this has been accurate. Video conferencing technology has quickly become the norm and a critical business tool. Many businesses now operate client and colleague interactions as a hybrid face-to-face and video conferencing model.

In recent years, we have honed the ability to utilise scarce human resources through remote working. No longer do businesses need super-expensive office buildings in fixed locations to house their workforce and service their clients. A laptop, an internet con-nection and cloud accessibility, and there you have it... an instant office. This way of communicating has put a lot of time back into many people's working days. This is the case both in regional markets, where entrepreneurs have traditionally travelled many kilometres to service clients, and in urban environments, where people can spend much of their day frustratingly stuck in traffic or on public transport.

I have watched as one of my mentor clients, a project man-agement business, rapidly and successfully transitioned from start-up, to capacity, to scalable in an extraordinarily short time. The entrepreneur was able to facilitate this by leveraging project management tools that allowed him to capture his knowledge in a business system. This enabled his rapidly growing team to expand beyond localised markets and into broader geographic regions.

It's not just service businesses that have benefited. I work with a client who manufactures large-scale agricultural equipment. In exploring opportunities to expand into new global markets, we have met with some of the biggest manufacturing and distributing companies in the world. Although my client and I are over 250 kilometres apart and the parties we talk to are on the other side of the planet, through video conferencing we have been able to build genuine rapport. We have interviewed potential suitors and built meaningful relationships that have progressed opportunities without leaving our offices in regional Australia.

My executive assistant has been with me for four years now and I couldn't live without her. We talk daily and I rely heavily on her to run my world. Her tasks include managing my calendar, making diary appointments, answering my phone when I'm in meetings and confirming my schedule with clients. This critical, right-person right-job role enables me to leverage my precious time and spend more of it in service to my clients. I wanted a person who started work early in the morning – when I did – so I selected an EA who lives in New Zealand, which effectively gives me a two-hour head start on the day. I start work at 7am and my EA starts at 9am, but we start work together. Not only that, I recruited her through an online global jobbing platform by paying a small subscription fee, loading on a project brief that freelance workers from around the globe responded to, and voila, there she was.

Technology has removed significant constraints for many entrepreneurial businesses and provided access to human resource expertise like never before. All sorts of opportunities can open up and displace the market. These opportunities should, if deployed effectively, provide the entrepreneurial business with the ability to fill a niche offering that enables them to charge a premium price – a price that previously only large organisations could charge.

The growth constraints of geography, infrastructure and access to technology are not so real any more.

In Jim Collins' extraordinary business book, *Good to Great: Why Some Companies Make the Leap and Others Don't*, the author nominates 'technology accelerators' as one area of breakthrough for companies that make the leap to long-term sustainability. I am sure that in 2001, when the book was written, access to these was a significant challenge and created very real barriers to entry for SMEs. But today, with so many cheap, accessible applications, I would argue that this is no longer the case.

The accessibility and acceleration of technology over recent years has enabled the types of efficiencies that not long ago were prohibitive for entrepreneurial businesses. Access to game-changing technology has traditionally formed part of the challenge of breaking through the entrepreneurial ceiling and scaling. Musk (Tesla/Space X), Branson (Virgin) and Knight (Nike) all had to take extreme risks in accumulating sufficient resources to provide their businesses with the scale to compete effectively. Technology enabled by the subscription model should provide many of the tools that have traditionally been acquired through high-risk gambles, which historically have been a prerequisite to significant scalability.

With a well thought through strategic displacement game plan, your entrepreneurial business can leverage tools that have never before been available or have financially been out of reach. Combined with agile, fast decision making, the ability to work directly with clients and understand their needs, as well as the tools to understand and access larger, more remote markets without setting up commercial property, this creates a favourable entrepreneurial storm. Potentially a perfect storm where entrepreneurial creativity is enabled through business systems and structures. A perfect storm to break through the entrepreneurial ceiling.

The road from chaos and overwhelm, and through the entrepreneurial ceiling to create rewarding, impactful enterprises, has never been more accessible.

It is a highly rewarding journey that should feed your entrepreneurial thirst for creativity and adventure, while mitigating and systemising tasks you do not enjoy or are not particularly good at.

Creating a business by design is a journey of exploration. It is at times a highly creative, rewarding process, and at other times requires great discipline and structure. The journey takes you on an emotional roller coaster that challenges you daily to lift your eyes out of the weeds and lock on to a bigger picture of a scalable and rewarding business. Making the decision to break through the entrepreneurial ceiling and climb the ladder through transformational sustainability is, like Alice entering Wonderland, at times exciting, at times mundane, at times exhilarating and at times terrifying. It's all part of the deal and, as an entrepreneur who has lived life porpoising under the entrepreneurial ceiling, when all is said and done, you probably wouldn't have it any other way.

BREAKTHROUGH
BITES

While you believe your path is unique and yours alone to tread, this is simply not true. Your path has been walked many millions of times before.

Although your products differ, your leadership styles differ and your businesses differ, there is a similarity, consistency and pattern in the journeys that entrepreneurs take, and many have taken that journey before you.

The entrepreneurial journey is punctuated by the highest of highs and the lowest of lows. The fortunes of the business can wildly fluctuate based on the energy of you, the entrepreneur.

The entrepreneurial ladder has three rungs below the entrepreneurial ceiling:

1. Start-up
2. High-Growth
3. Capacity

The entrepreneurial ladder has three rungs above the entrepreneurial ceiling:

1. Transformational
2. Consistent
3. Scalable

- You will be condemned to a business life below the entrepreneurial ceiling unless you can truly change the way you do business and how you operate.

- Small businesses that act like big businesses invariably become big businesses.

- Accessible technology is a game changer for SMEs looking to execute a displacement strategy.

- The road beyond chaos and overwhelm and through the entrepreneurial ceiling to create rewarding, impactful enterprises has never been more accessible to those who decide to set out on this quest.

- A displacement strategy where you change the rules on how you operate has never been more possible for SME businesses than it is today.

2

Prepare to Launch

Beyond chaos and overwhelm

As you commence your journey through the entrepreneurial ceiling, it can be useful to understand how others have done it, gain some perspective on the likelihood that you will succeed and prepare for what is ahead.

The wine industry is a very challenging industry. It is highly competitive and requires extensive business and technical expertise. I have worked with many wineries, but in recent years have worked with one winery intensively as they look to transition through the entrepreneurial ceiling.

Many of us open a bottle of wine with little thought about how it was produced or the business that made it happen. If you're running a winery, you are running a very complex business. You generally have a vineyard, along with all the challenges of an agricultural enterprise. High rainfall, low rainfall, disease, drought, not enough water, too much water, frosts, pests, plagues, chemicals, capital investment in expensive machinery, fertiliser, irrigation infrastructure and vine infrastructure, not to mention dwindling labour options. Then there is the timing of it all. The to-the-minute assessment of when the various grape varieties are ready to be picked and the challenges of aligning resources to make this happen at short notice. At harvest time (called 'vintage' in the industry), it's all hands on deck and one wrong move can see the whole crop, and your seasonal livelihood, ruined.

Once you have achieved the minor miracle of getting the grapes picked, the business focus moves to manufacturing. This requires a very different skill set that, through some sort of magical process, transforms the humble grape into a sophisticated, alcohol-laden product.

As a winemaker you must be part scientist and part artist, as the subtlest of tweaks have significant impacts. From stemming the grapes, to crushing, fermenting, filtering, cellaring and ultimately bottling them, there are critical decisions to be made to ensure the wine has the quality to represent the history and lineage of its label. No pressure!

Then there is the retail arm – a vibrant, buzzing cellar door filled with laughing, happy people. Cellar door experts deftly lead the budding wine connoisseurs through the product range to ensure that they understand the complexities of the wine they're sampling. It's a delightful meander through the different styles, varietals and regional characteristics.

Finally, you must master the wholesale arm of the business. A dog-eat-dog, competitive market where the balance between volume sales and price premium is critical. A world where brand is everything and history counts. This world has a number of external players to support your distribution that form the bridge between the winery and retail stockists, food service venues, restaurants and cafés.

That is just the product development, manufacturing and distribution. There is also the business management to consider. This is the element of the business that joins the dots between the different needs and wants of each division and miraculously creates commercial outcomes. Cash flow projections, pricing models, export and compliance, sales and marketing, promotions and campaigns, events, tastings, tourism familiarisations and, of course, the most challenging of all for many – managing the people stuff.

This is a complex business model that ebbs and flows with the seasons and is highly susceptible to external influences and events. You would think that managing so many moving parts would be quite enough for any entrepreneur, but in recent years my client has had to contend with so much more.

The summer of 2019-20 was hot. Most days hovered around 40 °C and the high country near my client's business was ablaze. During that summer an area the size of Tasmania was destroyed by wild fires. For most of that season the region was thick with smoke that stung your eyes, fouled your clothes and made it difficult to breathe outdoors. Unfortunately, this was also a critical time in the vineyard as the grapes were ripening on the vine. The risk of smoke taint – which could render the crop unsuitable for wine making and effectively wipe out a whole year's income, not to mention the associated costs to grow and harvest the crop – hung over the business. It was a potential financial disaster happening before our eyes!

As days turned to weeks the hope that the crop would be okay faded. The courageous owners never gave up believing that the crop would be salvageable, but this was not to be. It was heart-breaking. Smoke taint changed the chemical composition of the grapes and rendered the juice useless for wine making. The entire season had been lost.

By February 2020 the blaze was extinguished, and the region had become the focus of world attention that sparked an outpouring of generosity and support. Little did my client know that their woes would not end here.

In March 2020, four weeks later, a new threat emerged. COVID-19 struck. The business would go on to endure two years of lockdowns. Overnight their direct-to-consumer market, which was a significant element of their income stream, totally evaporated. The worry, concern and guilt was palpable as they struggled with the potential loss of 145 years of family winemaking.

They say things come in threes, and as if this wasn't enough, there was one more blow on the horizon. A few months after COVID lockdowns began. The Chinese government mandated an embargo on Australian wine, which saw sixteen per cent of the business's distribution disappear overnight. Oh, my goodness. Could this really be happening?!

A resilient, talented and dynamic mother and daughter team run this family business – the seventh generation to do so. This is remarkable when you consider that neither mother nor daughter is a winemaker. Given this, they face more challenges than traditional wine businesses in which the winemaker is the entrepreneur.

This business has followed the same path as many other entrepreneurial businesses, operating on a fragile combination of hard work, long hours, passion and key-person knowledge. While some business systems and processes have evolved over many years of operation, these were rarely documented. The business has existed in a whirlwind of activity, with the owners and often the team in a constant state of exhaustion. They have jumped from one seasonal crisis to the next, totally reactive to whatever was coming at them. This was dramatically amplified across the summer and autumn of 2020.

It is difficult to part ways with such tradition and history but, after seven generations, what got this business to today was not going to get them through tomorrow. It was time to change and get the mindset, structures, processes and people in place to break through the entrepreneurial ceiling, create a business by design and rewrite the story. The challenge, of course, is where to start with such a complex business model. Well, the starting point is the creation of an inspirational vision of what they wanted their business of the future to look and feel like. They committed to a new direction! Despite facing unprecedented adversity and external factors totally beyond their control, they made the decision to do things differently. This break with tradition was a big deal, given the extraordinary lineage, history and baggage that comes with seven generations of history.

I recently heard a wonderful keynote speech from Alexia Hilbertidou, one of New Zealand's most inspirational young leaders and the youngest ever winner of a Queen's Young Leader Award. Alexia founded a program called Girl Boss[1] to get more girls into information technology and STEM programs in schools. She said,

> *'If you want opportunities that not many people get, you need to make choices that not many people make.'*

I think this is a wonderful mantra for an entrepreneur who wants to break through the entrepreneurial ceiling and create a business by design. It takes courage, commitment and belief. Belief is fostered through action and realised by doing what most people will not. The status quo of being trapped under the entrepreneurial ceiling can be chaotic and often overwhelming, but nonetheless it is familiar. Staying trapped requires little courage; committing to do things differently requires daring.

In the 2022 AFL season Geelong Football Club did it differently. The oldest team to ever play a game in AFL history attracted significant criticism for resting key older players throughout the season in a bid to have them primed for the finals series. But it worked!

Following Geelong's demolition of Sydney in the Grand Final, coach Chris Scott said, 'It's a metaphor for life really, if you want to do great things, don't expect it to be smooth sailing. You're going to have to shake hands with adversity at some point. If you hang in, with no guarantee that you'll get the ultimate success, it might be worth it.'

The good news, however, is that mustering the courage to be

different is not new to you. After all, there was a time that you started or took on a business and backed yourself to follow your dream. It is this feeling you must again capture. So, what's holding you back now? Would it help if I told you that you had the odds in your favour?

You may have heard unsubstantiated claims bandied around about failure rates of SMEs, but believe it or not, the statistics for SME sustainability in Australia are very healthy.

Are the numbers we hear around SME failure real?

There are lots of statistics thrown around about how many small businesses fail and how often. I have heard that four out of five small businesses fail in the first five years, and four out of five fail in the next five years. Many of these 'truths' have materialised from urban myths. To understand the real numbers, I thought I might check out the actual statistics with the Australian Bureau of Statistics[2] and yes, the numbers are frightening.

In Australia, as of 30 June 2021, there were 2,402,254 actively trading businesses. In the four financial years from 2017–18 to 2020–21, there were 1,128,355 business exits. That's an average per annum of 282,089. This means that approximately 12% of businesses fail each year, and over the fabled five-year period approximately 59% of businesses fail.

The statistics, of course, don't reveal why these businesses exited, but I suspect the overwhelm of running an entrepreneurial enterprise below the ceiling will have a reasonable representation in the numbers. The good news is that Australians are also an adventurous lot. In the same four-year period cited above, a whopping 1,392,813 businesses entered the market. In fact, in this period Australia experienced a net gain of 264,458 businesses.

Business entries and exits, 2017-18 to 2020-21, Australia (000s)

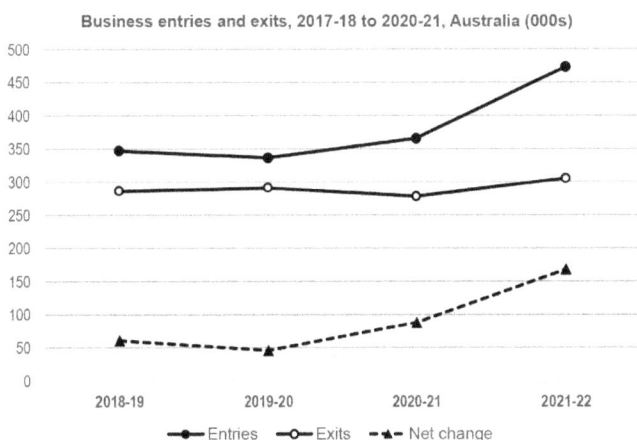

So, what does this really mean?

Clearly the tale of doom and gloom built around small business failure does not tell the whole story. It turns out that of the 277,674 businesses that exited in 2021, 272,282 turned over less than $2 million and 83% of these turned over less than $200,000. It is clear from this data that all business exits are not equal, and the facts are that: **if your business turns over more than $200,000, you have an 82% chance of survival year to year. If your revenue exceeds $2,000,000 per annum, you have a 98% chance of survival year on year.** The odds of survival over a journey are actually pretty good!

There are any number of meanings we can attach to this data, but the one I think is most useful is that you can afford to be brave as an SME as the odds are in your favour. The fear-mongering that has permeated our psyche through myths and legends of small business failure does not stack up when we look at the facts.

> *As we begin the journey of breaking through the entrepreneurial ceiling and moving from chaotic and overwhelmed to scalable and rewarding, we can gain comfort from the fact that the stories of failure are not supported by the numbers.*

Our natural evolutionary bias, thanks to our cave-dwelling ancestors, will continually remind us that failure is imminent if we stray from the path. But as we have seen, the facts don't support this story.

Start with why

The shift successful entrepreneurs make that enables them to create extraordinary businesses is that they take the time to think through why they do what they do, and how it aligns with their larger purpose. It's often useful to reflect on when we started or acquired our business, and ask what it was that we were looking to achieve and why. What purpose did it serve to take the leap?

In your current business context, the why can produce profound insights into a more effective business model. Why do we compete the way we do in the markets we serve? What if we were to diversify into more profitable, less competitive markets? What if we build this capability to drive into that market? Learn to take the time to explore and consider. Work on the business, not just in it as the technician. Take yourself beyond the role of an employee and position yourself as a leader with a why and a purpose others would want to follow.

So many of you short-cut the why in favour of the how, and there is good reason for this. The how is the natural bias to activity that has served you, the entrepreneur, so well. There is no shortage of 'how' for creative people. But if you start at the how, without considering the why and the broader purpose of what you wish to achieve, it will be difficult to progress your transformation and breakthrough. You are likely to burn considerable resources, enact change fatigue in your people and damage business confidence – most notably your own.

It is in knowing the why before embarking on the how – by deliberately creating strategic goals and tactical clarity, then unleashing your entrepreneurial bias to act – that you can commence transformation and truly build a business by design that gives you the lifestyle, freedom and choice you crave.

By doing what most people do – that is, looking to implement a whole raft of creative brain bubbles willy nilly without actually considering how they will affect your journey through the entrepreneurial ceiling and how they will service your greater purpose – you are likely to do more harm than good.

Brain bubbles, implemented on the run and without alignment to a greater purpose, are unlikely to get the buy-in of the team. A strategic framework that has little understanding of how it contributes to breakthrough will just be tinkering and add another burdensome thing to your already overwhelmed existence. Brain bubbles, although well intentioned, if not part of a broader strategic game plan, are likely to confuse your people, burn precious time, erode resources and badly affect culture and confidence.

Abraham Lincoln famously said, 'Give me six hours to chop down a tree and I will spend the first four sharpening the axe.' The message is clear: stop being busy being busy, take the time to get your strategic aspiration aligned with your purpose, and stop hacking away at your business with a blunt axe.

My favourite saying from the Greek philosopher Socrates is, 'The secret of change is to focus all your energy not on fighting the old, but on building the new.' If you can focus your energy and attention on the greater why and align your aspiration and strategic direction with your purpose, you are in the right place to have a meaningful tilt at breakthrough and building a business by design.

Back to our seventh-generation winery: today they are well on their way to creating a business by their design structured around the vision they have laid out before them.

Having survived a period of extraordinary adversity, they set out on a path of renewal. They have defined roles and responsibilities aligned with their strengths and expertise. They have implemented new software programs that drive direct online sales, and in doing so bolstered their direct-to-consumer category. They have implemented new financial software that reports on metrics and informs data-driven decision making by the management team. They have undertaken capital expenditure and re-engineered the winery to create efficiencies and increased productivity through the manufacturing process, and in doing so pulled costs out of the business. They have engaged an HR company that has supported them to build sustainable people structures and processes. They have designed a robust governance structure with a senior management team that is heavily involved in decision making, and appointed an independent chair to provide oversight, insight and experience. They have hired a new and contemporary marketing manager, who has implemented a luxury look and feel to the brand and products while developing a community of fortified wine connoisseurs to share their experiences and love of fortified wines.

Having lived and survived through the extraordinary period of calamity that was the summer of 2020, my clients understand that uncertainty is part of the game of business and have embraced the lessons it brings. A strong why and clearly defined purpose sit at the core of everything they do. They have faced extraordinary external events and stared them down, one after another, with steely determination. They have shaken hands with adversity. As a result, they have emerged from each challenge better, wiser, stronger and more resilient.

The battle is ongoing and the complexity of the business model creates multiple layers of challenge that must be addressed day to day, week to week and season to season. They have achieved an incredible amount of change in a relatively short period. They have not rested on their history or standing in the industry but, rather, have taken the road less travelled and looked to break through the entrepreneurial ceiling, transform their business, and build a business and life by design for themselves and their people.

As the entrepreneur of an SME you must make choices, and they are your choices to make. You can keep waiting for Bill Murray's Groundhog Day alarm clock to wake you every day, turn up to a job and wish that things would change. Or you can do things differently. By clearly understanding your why, leveraging your propensity to act and steeling yourself to lean into the uncomfortable, you will be in a great position to commence your transformation and break through the entrepreneurial ceiling.

BREAKTHROUGH
BITES

- If you want opportunities that not many people get, you need to make choices that not many people make.

- As we begin the journey of breaking through the entrepreneurial ceiling and moving from chaotic and overwhelmed to scalable and rewarding, we can gain comfort from knowing that the stories of failure are not supported by the numbers.

- In order to achieve great things that are worthwhile, you will invariably have to shake hands with adversity.

- Nothing worthwhile comes easily, and it is in leaning into discomfort that we prepare ourselves for what lies ahead.

- It is in knowing the why before embarking on the how, facilitated through the deliberate creation of strategic goals and tactical clarity, that enables you to unleash your entrepreneurial bias to act.

- 'Give me six hours to chop down a tree and I will spend the first four sharpening the axe.' Abraham Lincoln.

- 'The secret of change is to focus all your energy, not on fighting the old, but on building the new.' Socrates.

3

Set an Inspirational Strategy

A winning aspiration

The starting point for breaking through to the transitional business lifecycle and commencing our journey is to design and create a big aspirational idea on which we can set our sights. To truly commit to change and inspire us to lean in, even in the hardest of times, we must set an aspiration so clear, so compelling and so inspiring that any course of action that could derail our path is dwarfed by the vision ahead.

The vision must be tangible, so that when we are in the day-to-day operational weeds and can't see our way through, we have a mechanism and process to regain perspective and recalibrate. We can take a moment, lift our heads above the weeds and take a big gulp of future aspiration. This will allow us to re-attach to the emotion and feeling of future self before we dive back into reality and the daily work that must get done.

Jim Collins, in his book *Good to Great*, called these aspirations 'big, hairy audacious goals'. Goals that '...are conceivable but of such magnitude and significance that they inspire us as leaders to strive in the day to day and moment to moment to be daring and continue our climb no matter how painful it is, no matter how far away our aspiration seems.'

Strategic inspiration is not a set and forget process. The business environment has a nasty habit of changing the rules, changing the playing conditions and changing the game. Nonetheless, the ability to adjust (termed 'pivot' during COVID), recalibrate and realign your aspirations is critical if you are to stay the path and break through the entrepreneurial ceiling.

In a small rural town in southern New South Wales, an SME engaged me to write a strategic plan and mentor the son of the owner, who was in his early twenties. The company manufactured structural steel for commercial buildings and had a state government contract to build the body of Rural Fire Service vehicles. The business also served local farmers with many of their agricultural needs. The factory showroom was set up as an industrial rural supplies shop, which also sold small farm machinery. The business had approximately eighteen employees and was the biggest employer in the district.

Not long after I was engaged, the business suffered a significant blow. In 2010 we received news that the Rural Fire Service contract was not going to be renewed. The revenue from this contract was significant and the overheads and capital expenditure that the business had committed to meant it was geared to achieve a revenue number that included the Rural Fire Service contract.

The main artery of the business, the structural steel division, was also being challenged. This division had grown dramatically after the 2008 financial crisis, when a government stimulus program pumped a lot of money into the sector. As the stimulus money dried up and projects were completed, structural steel became a highly competitive, price-driven market. It was extremely difficult to make money in the industry and this business was no exception.

At the end of 2014, struggling for cash and limping along, an environmental scan brought home some ugly truths. The structural steel industry was unlikely to get the business where it needed to go. At its heart and soul, the company was an agricultural original equipment manufacturer (OEM). It was time to get back to its roots.

The first plan, written in 2010, had been somewhat business as usual with the addition of the development of chaser bins (grain carts that follow behind the harvester and transport grain so the harvester does not have to stop), mostly in response to the loss of the Rural Fire Service contract. By 2014, chaser bin demand had increased significantly and now contributed a sizeable chunk of the revenue and an even greater component of the profit. To create this division, the business had embarked on a significant capital investment program, which had seen the purchase of important infrastructure and capital equipment along with the introduction of robust systems and reporting mechanisms. The shift to a product-based business model supported by these pivotal tools would lay the foundations of the company's future. It was at this point the young mentoree was appointed general manager, and the succession of the business commenced.

The second plan was written in 2015, and saw the business invest heavily in building new manufacturing sheds of the massive scale required to handle the size of the huge chaser bins. The new plan was dynamic and bold. Infrastructure, people, market penetration and capital aligned behind a big hairy audacious, but focused, goal that would drive the future direction of the organisation. Significant investment was made in reinvigorating the brand, and money was pumped into digital marketing. The retail front of the facility was closed, and the space fitted out as brand-new offices. The business hired an HR manager, a CFO and an operations manager. A sales team was employed that covered every inch of Australia to mitigate the impact of drought. While drought was a serious business risk, the whole of Australia had never been in drought at the same time. The aspiration was driving the behaviour as well as focusing the investment, and the business boomed.

As the business entered 2017, it was growing, profitable and dynamic. It was ably led by its relatively young general manager with his father and owner as the managing director. The products had won significant and prestigious industry awards. Market acceptance had been strong, with the products positioned as the BMW of agricultural equipment. There was high demand. The workforce was united, proud of the company and working closely with the management team to continually improve. There was even a company bus that brought many employees to work every day from a nearby town. The strategy was working!

The winter drought of 2017 was like nothing Australia had seen before. A drought normally comes on in spring and summer, but this drought was different. This drought affected every corner of the country and would last nearly two long agonising years. Demand for chaser bins dried up along with the land and the failing crops. By the summer of 2017, it was clear things were going to get tough. The cashflow dried up with the paddocks, and by the time the drought broke in 2019 the business had been almost destroyed. Still functioning but on financial life support, the company started the long slow climb towards recovery, as did the client base.

The drought and subsequent two-year period were highly traumatic. The intense stress of managing the day to day was like dangling from a cliff face holding on by your fingertips. During this time, the strategy to put all of their eggs in one basket and shift the business to fully align with the agriculture sector was questioned. Everything that was known about how droughts occurred and played out, which had been the backbone of the geographic expansion strategy, was now obsolete. What we knew for sure no longer held true.

Following the drought, the business gradually returned to health and was able to rebuild its people and finances, but the scares of that time remained. Having reset their aspiration away from structural steel and fully aligned with the domestic agricultural sector, the business was in jeopardy. By the time COVID hit in March 2020, the business had recovered and was trading well. It was time for a new plan: plan three.

This plan was different from the other two. Plan three was very big, very hairy and very audacious. It was incredibly aspirational and would take the previous learnings and mould them into a compelling game plan. It looked to extend the business reach globally, diversify into new markets, increase manufacturing capacity and build the capability of the company's people and leaders. This plan would be a game changer ... again!

Mike Tyson, the notorious boxer, said, 'Everyone has a plan, until they get punched in the mouth.'

I am sure there is an element of truth here; however, each stage of the evolution of this business has been built on the foundations of the previous stage. Even in the toughest of times, the business was able to adapt, learn and survive. The role of the strategic plan was not to predict the future, but rather plot it within circumstantial tolerances that were beyond the business's control.

Alex Hagan, in his book *Thriving in Complexity*, defines strategy as 'a high-level plan to achieve one or more goals under conditions of uncertainty'. He then notes that, 'many [businesses] forget about the conditions of uncertainty part of that definition of strategy and build a strategy based on today's business environment.' This business had experienced conditions of uncertainty firsthand and it was a lesson well learned.

While the determined triumph over adversity is inspirational, the real story is a very personal one of evolving and transformational leadership. When the general manager was young and inexperienced and the business was flying high, all roads, decisions and processes went through him. But not any more, and it is no fluke that this is no longer the case. Each strategic plan has gradually built capability in the team and the processes to release the entrepreneurial shackles. It has facilitated transitional progression through the entrepreneurial ceiling towards a scalable, family-corporate business model.

The evolution of strategic thinking

Blue Ocean Strategy is a book that has resonated with business leaders around the world. It has sold over four million copies and been printed in forty-four languages. Its authors, W. Chan Kim and Renee Mauborgne (Professors at University of Michigan), introduced the blue ocean concept in a *Harvard Business Review* (HBR) article in 2004[3].

Business strategy at that time followed a very structured process. It went along the lines of: assess the industry and environment in which the business operates; determine the competition within this environment and identify strengths and weaknesses; then set about identifying a distinctive competitive advantage around how to compete. Align supply chain, marketing and human resources, then model this up into a financial budget.

The underpinning assumption was that business strategy is bound by the environment in which it operates. They called this a 'structuralist' approach to developing strategy. It is a view that says the outcomes, and indeed success, of your strategic intent is based on the ability of the organisation to successfully exploit environmental circumstances, rather than the ability of the organisation to undertake game-changing strategies that might shift the industry.

While a structuralist approach has been historically effective in developing strategic plans, I prefer a more aspirational methodology – a process in which you plot your own path and look to shift the playing field of your industry. And it appears Chan Kim and Mauborgne agree.

The authors talk about the success of Griffith-based wine company Casella Wines in shifting the American wine market. Casella created a sweeter, more easy drinking wine that had mass market appeal. This moved the perception of a typical wine drinker away from the swirl and sniff elite who have training and expertise in the appreciation of fine wine. In the HBR article, the basic premise was that the ideas and actions of individual players could shape the industries in which they operate. They called this approach 'reconstructionist'.

Indeed, since this article was written a few years ago, we have seen the emergence of companies that have dramatically reshaped and created industries and industry sectors and gone on to top the S&P 500. The products and platforms produced by leading companies such as Apple, Google and Amazon either did not exist in their current form when this article was written, or were in their infancy. It seems extraordinary, given how ubiquitous they are today, that the first iPhone was only introduced in 2007.

In looking at the evolution of the most successful global companies and brands, it's hard to argue with Chan Kim and Mauborgne. The top five list is dominated by companies that have revolutionised their industries and worked outside environmental boundaries and known competitive conditions. They have introduced game-changing technologies, ideas and ways of working that have infiltrated every aspect of our lives. It's the classic guys and girls in the garage modus operandi. Small businesses that have played like big businesses have ultimately become big businesses.

The tools and processes for determining corporate strategy in the 80s and 90s, which were championed by management gurus like Drucker and Porter, are still useful for gaining perspective and understanding the world in which we compete. However, as stand-alone strategic tools, they are found wanting in a modern competitive business environment.

> *Modern strategic thinking, as highlighted by the most successful brands in the world, should, in theory, play into the hands of agile, highly responsive and creative entrepreneurs.*

The cruel paradox is, however, that the very traits that help our wonderful entrepreneurs achieve lift-off and growth will often contribute to their downfall as demand outstrips supply and companies find themselves at capacity. Unless you can move past the porpoising rung of the entrepreneurial ladder, you may find yourself stuck in a time warp where chaos and overwhelm abound.

It can be difficult to translate the strategic lessons, theories, initiatives and concepts applicable to an S&P 500 company to the less well-resourced entrepreneurial business striving towards a scalable business model. Having said that, I would argue that effective and practical strategic planning is even more critical in your business, given that your business has limited economies of scale compared with industry behemoths and limited access to scarce resources. It is critical that you have access to practical, action-based strategic planning tools that set future direction and guide decision making.

It is through deliberately deciding to do things differently in an SME environment of limited resources that you will be able to achieve breakthrough.

Strategic planning is the process that will enable you to set your future direction and align your resources and capabilities with your aspiration. A winning aspiration that will define your future direction and inspire action. Having control of where and how you compete circumvents the historical methodology of examining environmental conditions and what others are doing, which potentially narrows vision and stifles creativity.

In assessing strategic planning successes and failures over many years, I have found that three key characteristics have emerged. While this is not a book on crafting strategic plans, if you are going to have an impactful vision for your business and invest the time to write a strategic plan, you may as well ensure that it has the key elements that give it every chance to survive the first punch.

Recognise compounding

I believe you are where you are today because of the experiences you have accumulated on the journey and the lessons these experiences have provided. If you look back over your journey and career, just like a join-the-dots puzzle, you can see the sliding door moments that contributed to both the stagnation and acceleration of your business and personal journey.

Interestingly, in hindsight you can see that the moments that are most defining probably occurred when you felt most challenged.

The night is darkest before the dawn. Your journey is the cumulative effect of all these experiences, and I truly believe that everything you have strived to achieve – successful or otherwise – has got you where you are today. I call this effect compounding. Like the compounding of interest that, little by little, sees your retirement fund grow. The same is true for you and your business.

Compounding of knowledge and resources in a business is a critical element of business success.

Running a business is a path littered with challenges and punctuated by both high and low moments. We get caught in the short-term cycle of measuring business success but, ultimately, this is not what will define our journey.

Again, your hardwiring and evolutionary bias is not your friend when it comes to getting your head around the power of compounding. You naturally choose short-term reward over long-term benefit. As an evolutionary tool, where a kill-and-eat mentality was essential for survival, this was an imperative. But in today's world, this does not necessarily serve you well. Your natural inclinations are to satisfy short-term rewards, and in the absence of a compelling longer-term vision there is no framework that we can lean on to resist these urges.

Your health is an excellent example of this evolutionary instinct at play in the modern world. Without a predetermined long-term vision of what we want to become, eating that take away food or putting off that gym session is easily done. After all, we go to the gym, lift weights for an hour and ... nothing changes. But when we lift weights three times a week for over a year, miracles happen.

Another evolutionary bias that is against us is the bias towards quick wins. That is, a lack of progression in the very short term doesn't sit well with us. To get a better handle on the impacts of compounding, let's have a look at the following scenario.

If I put one cent in a jar on day one of the month and double the amount I put into the jar every day, I will have amassed $5,368,709.12 by the thirtieth day. This is a staggering number when you consider I had started with one cent and incredibly difficult to get your head around. On day ten, a third of the way through, I would have $10.24. By day twenty things are getting interesting, with my jar having $5,242.88 in it, but that is still only 1% of the total I would climb to in another ten days' time. The last ten days is when all the magic happens, but without the initial period of slow growth, and indeed making a start in the first place, this would never transpire.

We have all heard about the overnight success story that, when explored deeper, turns out to involve years of working towards the breakthrough. Like these compounding examples, the best-laid plans need time to ride the bumps of short- and medium-term events to be successful. We need to accumulate enough learning and experience to affect the day to day, but over time the compounding effects of these lessons and experience will form the foundations of our business by design.

Build in redundancy

I am a huge fan of Scott Pape, better known as the Barefoot Investor. Starting with a nationally syndicated newspaper article in the early 2000s, by 2017 he had written his bestselling book by the same name. *The Barefoot Investor* is a brilliant how to guide to getting out of debt and creating personal wealth. Because entrepreneurial family-based businesses are so intertwined with personal financial management, the lessons Pape teaches translate perfectly to many elements of successful SME businesses.

The concepts are simple, but not necessarily easy. According to Pape, one of the key ingredients in getting out of debt is finding your mojo. Mojo, for him, is the savings account separated from your day to day spend that provides peace of mind and a financial back-up when unexpected troubles occur.

To me, having a mojo back-up makes sense in a business

environment as well. It is very difficult to be creative, innovative and energised in your business when you're surrounded by bills. Pape advocates paying up and chopping up credit cards, living within your means and keeping to a budget. Sound advice both personally and in business. While this may not be totally practical for businesses, especially those that live in fluctuating demand cycles, the redundancy message around having a fallback position when things don't go the way we expect is right on the money.

We have all heard the story of the entrepreneur who risked it all to amass a fortune, but we rarely hear of the entrepreneur who risked it all and failed despite the fact they are considerably more common than those that have struck it rich.

Thomas Edison[4] was one of the industrial world's first entrepreneurs. He was credited for inventing the light bulb (not true, it had been around for some time, but he did invent the vacuum and filament that made it reliable and efficient), and also invented and patented the entire electricity system that powered the light bulb; the first motion picture device; the electronic vote recorder; an iron ore separator; and his favourite invention, the phonograph.

The phonograph was considered his first invention, which he patented at the age of twenty-two while working as a telegraph operator. The machine was able to record the spoken voice and play it back. Speaking into a receiver caused a needle to vibrate and make indentations in a drum covered in tin foil. The first recorded message was Edison reciting 'Mary had a Little Lamb'. Edison developed the product and eventually used a wax covered needle to cut records and a hand-cranked machine to play them.

Edison also created the world's first record company in 1877. The business grew steadily, but the products relied on a highly secret wax to create the records, which became scarce when World War I broke out. The business model had no redundancy and had not innovated beyond the wax product. Many other record companies were also emerging at this time. Despite the fact that music and records were hugely popular during the roaring twenties era that followed the war, Edison's business never fully recovered and closed its doors in 1929.

Recent history is littered with examples of celebrity entrepreneurs who have come close to running out of money and having to close their doors. In 1962 Phil Knight was a student at Stanford University. He was taking a class on entrepreneurship as part of his MBA and was also a keen middle distance runner. He couldn't find shoes that were suitable for running and wrote a paper outlining a business idea to import running shoes. The idea for Nike was born, and the paper got an A.

In his compelling book about the history of Nike, *Shoe Dog*, Knight talks about the lack of redundancy built into his business model and the many moments when he thought the business was about to fold. For the first seven years the business (then called Blue Ribbon) was a shoe trader that imported Japanese shoes and totally relied on a third-party supplier. In 1971 the partnership went sour, in part due to disagreements around payment terms – Knight was scraping together the funds to pay for each shipment. It was then that Knight was forced to go it alone, and Nike was born.

In 1975 the business was funded through a line of credit with Japanese company Nissho Iwai, which in turn secured the backing of the Bank of California. Nissho could withdraw support at any time, so paying them on time was essential to Blue Ribbon's sustainability. At one point, when a cheque from a retailer was late, Blue Ribbon was $75,000 short of the $1 million they had to pay Nissho and were in danger of defaulting. To meet this payment, the bank accounts of Blue Ribbon's four retail stores, along with their factory in the UK, were emptied. As a result, the factory workers' pay cheques bounced. Disaster was narrowly averted when Knight leaned on a box supplier and borrowed enough to pay the workers.

Following this, the Bank of California removed their support for the second time in five years, and the revolving credit that floated the business came crashing down. Like the game of musical chairs, when the music stopped, Blue Ribbon was left standing. The FBI were notified of a possible fraud, and Knight believed he was going to jail. The business had no redundancy and had leveraged its growth beyond what was reasonable. It had been built on a financial house of cards.

Against all odds, the business was bailed out by Nissho Iwai, and the partnership went on to become one of the world's most successful sporting goods companies.

While these examples make for great stories, it is easy to see that the most likely scenario is that the businesses will fail, and that has been the case for many entrepreneurs. Growth costs money and cashflow is critical to sustaining growth. A key element of any entrepreneurial business model must be to retain a position of some redundancy, with a Plan B to account for unforeseen events.

Although we have no idea what form these events may take, history says they will happen. Most entrepreneurs will not be as lucky as Musk and Knight. Most, like Edison, will find the business unsustainable and terminal.

It is prudent to have an element of redundancy and conservatism in a plan if it is going to ride the bumps.

Be optimistic

In an article published in *Science Direct*[5] that drew on a wide range of works, Professor Tali Sharot of the University College of London looked at how optimistic humans generally are and what were the consequences of this. The study found that, 'When it comes to predicting what will happen to us tomorrow, next week, or fifty years from now, we overestimate the likelihood of positive events, and underestimate the likelihood of negative events.' Further, this 'optimism bias' is manifest in approximately 80% of the population. Professor Sharot went on to say:

> *'While classic theories in economics and psychology assert that correct beliefs will maximise reward and minimise loss, many sources of evidence point to the conclusion that optimism is nonetheless advantageous compared to unbiased predictions.'*

The absence of positive bias about the future is associated with mild depression and anxiety, which suggests that optimism is a key component of good mental health. And it doesn't end there. Turns out that optimism bias is also good for physical health.

> *'All else being equal, optimists live longer and are healthier. The effects can be quite substantial, with one survey of*

97,000 individuals reporting that optimists are 14% less
likely to die between the ages of 50 and 65, and 30%
less likely to die from cardiac arrest. Optimism has also
been related to extended survival time of cancer and
AIDS patients.'

What about other areas of life? Again, optimism bias is a very positive influence and 'appears to be related to success in the professional domain as well. Duke economists Puri and Robinson (2007) report that optimists work harder and longer hours, which may account for their higher pay.' Optimism has been linked to achievement in a broad range of fields, including education, business, sport and politics.

The natural inclination to value the present over the future is called temporal discounting. Interestingly, studies show that when optimistic expectations are abolished, these behaviours are reduced. 'This suggests that choosing to engage in an act that is rewarding at present but costly in the future (smoking, unprotected sex, overeating) can be partially explained by an excess of unrealistic optimism.'

The findings concluded:

'On balance, however, it seems that the benefits of unre-
alistic optimism may have outweighed the downfalls. The
biologists Ajit Varki (2009), Danny Brower and others have

argued that the evolution of mankind might have come to a halt without optimistic illusions.'

It appears optimism serves us well, but with a very strong caveat. In the absence of long-term vision and rewards, temporal discounting means we are likely to choose the option in the present that rewards us now.

In creating strategic inspiration that compounds your learning and history, builds in redundancy and gives you cause to be optimistic, you can ride the bumps, setbacks and challenges that arise in the day to day and moment to moment, and in doing so have the tools to stay the path.

This will give you strength and confidence in your direction. Confidence that will rub off on your people and those who are going with you. If you're going to go to this much effort, you might as well build in a few safeguards on the way. In doing so the ride will be smoother, the bumps will be a little less jarring and the catastrophes will be a little less catastrophic.

Craft an inspirational strategic plan

Remember, you are writing your plan to consider the various pitfalls and scenarios that may confront you on the journey, and to define a guiding aspiration that both you and your people can get behind. This should not be a weighty tome and does need to be a Pulitzer Prize winner. It *does* need to set the aspiration that will enable you to visualise what this thing will look like when you have broken through and are climbing the rungs of the entrepreneurial ladder, and what steps you will need to put in place in the day to day to make it happen.

In my workshops I use the 'Traction' method from the book of the same name by Gino Wickman. This process sets a ten-year goal, three-year picture, one-year plan and ninety-day rocks. It is a wonderful process to help you and your team envisage a future different from the one you are currently facing.

Creating your ten-year vision starts with visualising yourself in the world ten years from now. What are we driving? What will our homes look like? What could the market we play in look like? How will it have changed? What will our customers be looking for in our product or service, and how will we provide that? What revenue are we likely to make, how many people will we require, what will they be doing?

Next, the planning process takes the ten-year vision and crafts a three-year picture. This three-year picture will form the foundation for future growth. Again, the business questions you asked in developing your ten-year vision are relevant. But this time, the questions are prefaced with what we will we need to have achieved by the three-year mark to get to our ten-year vision.

Once the three-year picture has been crafted, we then go through the same process to draft our one-year game plan and ninety-day, big rock focus areas. The process concludes with identifying the issues that could block us that we must resolve to progress.

I have utilised the Traction process with many businesses, but one is a standout – an IT company that struggled to achieve long-term outcomes. It was highly reactive to what came at it. The organisational leaders as well as staff were totally overwhelmed and constantly operating in crisis mode. Since adopting the Traction model, this business has achieved remarkable success. By focusing diligently on long, medium- and short-term goals, as well as having the discipline to maintain the meeting and review structure, it has created a sustainable and successful business model that sets the aspiration and guides decision making in the day to day.

I have found this two-page Vision, Traction Organiser to be an incredibly powerful tool to focus entrepreneurial intent and activity. It is a tool that can be used in the day to day, and that will give perspective and help support optimism for the future for both you and your team. Staying the path can be difficult but, with one eye firmly planted on a very real and different future, the challenges in the day to day don't seem so insurmountable.

Back to our OEM...

We left our small regional OEM as they we were developing their new strategic plan. Twelve months on, a lot has changed.

The new plan has been the catalyst for a dramatic shift in the entrepreneurial owner. Inspired by a clear and bold new direction and hardened from the compounding effect of previous experiences, he has adopted a totally new leadership style.

His focus is now on building the capability of the leaders around him. Whereas before everything came through him and he bottlenecked many elements of the business, today he is confident in his team, his systems and his company's direction. He has built a wonderful team of skilled people around him and spent both time and resources on their development. It is a pillar of his plan.

The product has cracked the overseas market, and as we speak machines are landing in North America for product testing. He has identified and designed a machine that mimics the current machine, but can be used in a new application in a non-related industry. He has drought-proofed the business.

This business has punched through the entrepreneurial ceiling and is scaling dramatically. Systems-driven, leadership-capable, mitigated against the biggest risks, and with financial redundancy, the business is profitable. It has learned from past experiences and is compounding those lessons, and is optimistic and hopeful for the future.

This business has broken through. The owner, who is currently overseas proudly showing off his machines, is no longer over-whelmed, and the business is no longer chaotic. This business is well on the way to a sustainable, rewarding future where consistency is supported by systems and innovation driven by the team.

BREAKTHROUGH

BITES

- The starting point for breaking through to the transitional business lifecycle and commencing your journey through the entrepreneurial ceiling is to design and create a big aspirational idea on which you can set your sights.

- Having a defining inspirational strategy is important for the entrepreneurial leader, as it facilitates the building of capacity in the team and provides a different contextual perspective when times are tough.

- Modern strategic thinking, as highlighted by the most successful brands in the world, should play into the hands of agile, highly responsive and creative entrepreneurs.

- Deliberately deciding to do things differently in an SME environment is critical to achieve breakthrough.

- The absence of positive bias about the future is associated with mild depression and anxiety, which suggests that optimism is a key component of good mental health.

- Strategic planning is the process that will enable you to set your future direction and align your resources and capabilities with your aspiration.

- Compounding of knowledge and resources over time is a critical element of business success.

- The natural inclination to value the present over the future is called temporal discounting.

- It is prudent for you to have an element of redundancy and conservatism in any plan if it is going to ride the bumps.

4

Adopt a Breakthrough Attitude

A breakthrough attitude

Going through the entrepreneurial ceiling into a new world requires courage. You will need to let go of what you have known and what you have habitually done that creates certainty and safety. You will be wrestling with the knowledge that the business is neither ideal nor sustainable in the long term; however, it is providing an income and is a known commodity. The biggest barrier and challenge that you, the entrepreneur, face at this juncture is yourself. You are evolutionarily wired to be pessimistic and think the worst, and the fear of failure and losing all you have achieved loom large in the stories you tell yourself.

The big shift must come from within. The hardwired, ingrained evolutionary bias that once served you well, but today will be holding you back, must be overcome. You must counter a mindset that says, 'If I just work harder, all will be fine.' This mindset is a natural, but unhelpful default that takes away the need to face the uncertainty of a different future.

J. Pierpont Morgan[6] was an American financier who dominated Wall Street through the late 19th century and into the early 20th century. You may know his legacy company as JPMorgan Chase, which is worth $475.56 billion today. He said, 'The first step to getting somewhere is to decide that you are not going to stay where you are.' Sounds very simple, but having helped many entrepreneurs to break through the ceiling into a scalable business, I have found that this is indeed always the starting point. It's about individuals making the decision that where they are today is not where they want to be tomorrow.

> *This drive must be stronger than the uncertainty that precedes it.*

In Brené Brown's book *Daring Greatly,* and also Michael Dell's book *Play Fair but Win*, the authors quote the 1910 Theodore Roosevelt speech known as the Man in the Arena speech. This speech talks directly to the courage required to make the shift and dare greatly. Most people will have heard this or a version of it, but it goes:

'It is not the critic who counts, not the one who points out how the strong man stumbled or how the doer of deeds might have done them better. The credit belongs to the man who is actually in the arena, whose face is marred with sweat and dust and blood; who strives valiantly; who errs and comes short again and again; who knows the great enthusiasms, the great devotions, and spends himself in a worthy cause; who, if he wins, knows the triumph of high achievement; and who, if he fails, at least fails while daring greatly, so that his place shall never be with those cold and timid souls who know neither victory nor defeat.'

This speech talks to me in a slightly different way from both Brown and Dell. Rather than cheering for you, the man or woman in the arena, I am focused on the needs of your business. The business that so desperately requires you to take the leap of faith that will burst it through the ceiling and into the brave new world of the scalable, entrepreneurial business. Your business by design.

For the entrepreneur this is a very personal journey, and every person who has taken their business through the ceiling has done so by treading their own path. No one size will fit all, but know this: all great companies, at some point, have trodden this path. There is much to learn from those who have gone before us, both from those who have made it and, just as importantly, from those who have not.

> *'It is in your moments of decision
> that your destiny is shaped.'*
> *- Tony Robbins*

The moments of decision in the day to day are critical. The challenge is, however, that once you are in the moment, it is generally too late to work through what you should do. It is likely that eventually you will succumb to the path of least resistance, which is a sure-fire way to stay firmly wedged under the entrepreneurial ceiling.

To counter this, you must create a process to fall back on in moments of decision. Having a process to draw upon will enable you to take the right path. To delegate, look to a system fix or refer to a policy. These are all key indicators of a breakthrough business. When you are challenged and the old path of least resistance looks appealing, you will need to reframe the story you tell yourself and attach new meaning to tasks, challenges and problems that come at you in the day to day.

Initially, this new way of behaving will not come naturally to you. Entrepreneurs are wired for action and doing. Having watched entrepreneurs ping around the room for much of my career, I get that planning, management and being in the moment can be challenging for you. However, if you can recognise that you need to do things differently, and have a process to support that need, you can navigate through.

A not so seismic shift

> *'I know that success does not come at once,*
> *it is not a thing achieved overnight. It is*
> *the result of many, many, many years of*
> *working and trying to achieve goals.'*
>
> Novak Djokovic

Nothing worthwhile is easy, and it can take many years to become an overnight sensation. It fascinates me how, in so many ways, sport mirrors business. I know sport is not everyone's cup of tea but, nonetheless, the lessons we can take from competitive sport can help us improve our business performance. Take the story of tennis player Novak Djokovic's career, as told by Stephen Duneier in his 2017 Ted talk[7].

Djokovic began his tennis career in 2004. At this time, he was ranked 100+ in the world, his annual earnings were just over $US300,000 and he won 49% of all the tour matches he played. Interestingly, he also won 49% of the points in each match. When I facilitate workshops and play a pop quiz about these statistics, normally someone in the room will guess this number. It makes sense; the numbers align nicely and we are wired for patterns.

The next phase in Djokovic's career ran from 2006 to 2010. He had risen to number three in the world by this time, with annual earnings of $US5,000,000. He was now winning 79% of the matches he played. But although the winning percentage had risen by 30%, the percentage of points he won per match had not. To win 79% of matches, the points won had only increased by three per cent to 52%. Fun fact: rarely does anyone guess this statistic in my pop quiz, with the most common guess being 79%.

The last stage of Djokovic's career that Duneier examines is 2011 to 2016. Djokovic is number one in the world at this stage, with annual earnings of $US14,000,000. He is winning 90%, or nine out of ten, of the matches he plays. Fascinatingly and counter-intuitively, the percentage of points won has only increased a further three per cent to 55%.

How can a six per cent increase in points won equal a staggering $US13,700,000 in extra revenue and be the difference between a 100+ ranked player and the world number one?

If you are familiar with the game of tennis, it's easy to understand how this might occur. Djokovic could have won the points at the right times, that is, at break of serve. Or he could have outlasted his opponent over an exhausting five-set marathon because he remained mentally stronger as fatigue took over.

For me the answer lies off the court and in his preparation. I shudder to think how many tennis balls he hit on practice courts to build the strength, endurance and muscle memory required to prevail in key times throughout his matches. I can't imagine the sheer number of hours he must have spent in the gym to be so match hardened that when extreme fatigue set in, his body was able to withstand the pain and outlast his opponent. To endure such a gruelling training regimen, Djokovic must have had an unwavering belief that he would reach the pinnacle, and every tennis ball hit in practice inched him closer to his ultimate goal.

I liken this preparation to the entrepreneur's journey through the ceiling and on to breakthrough. Small, incremental steps applied in the moment inch the organisation ever closer to a scalable business model. Like Djokovic in the gym or on the practice court, no one set of reps or one particular ball hit in practice can be identified as the one that makes the difference. However, when collectively applied, these can lead to extraordinary outcomes. Ultimately for Djokovic, these compounding steps led to only an increase of six percent in his winning point ratio, but a massive winning ratio uplift of 41%.

The ability to take this journey in some form or another is critical to breaking through the entrepreneurial ceiling. It is not enough to make the decision to want to act differently as an organisation and as a leader, it is the action that follows that will determine the future course of the business. When you are trapped in the porpoising cycle of energy shifts and overwhelm, you must build and act on an inner determination to do things differently. This is often foreign work to you, the entrepreneur, and is not work you have traditionally valued.

There is no magic bullet to adopting a winning mindset, but there are some fundamentals that, if followed, will help you achieve breakthrough. You must do the work, get gritty, shift your self-talk and play to your natural proclivity to innovate and solve problems. Easier said than done, I hear you say, so let's explore each in turn with the aim of embedding them into your internal operating system so that, in times of stress and emergency, you can pull the red tag and inflate the life vest.

It's lonely at the top

Adopting a breakthrough attitude can be easier said than done. It is hard to make such significant change on your own, and it can be lonely at the top. Of course, working incredibly long hours and experiencing the stresses of running and operating a business are challenging in themselves, but for you, the entrepreneur, there is another factor at play that contributes to burnout and fatigue.

In June 2016 a French study was published on the psychological costs of owning and managing an SME[8]. The study collected data from 377 owner managers across a range of entrepreneurial businesses. One of the authors' key findings was that job stressors predict burnout through a feeling of occupational loneliness. In reading this finding, I could relate. Often my clients tell me, 'It's lonely at the top.' So not only do you, our intrepid entrepreneurial heroes, have to deal with ongoing customer demands, cashflow crises, business issues and staff problems, you also have to overcome a deep feeling of isolation as you try to work your way through an endless stream of challenges that can feel insurmountable.

If you are to create a business by design that is truly fulfilling, consistent and sustainable, it is critical that you get connected. Connecting with peers who run other entrepreneurial businesses is a great way to start. Industry associations that have networking events and help build connection with other entrepreneurs like yourself, who are facing similar challenges, can be a great source of inspiration, encouragement and confidence.

Another great way to combat loneliness at the top is to get a trusted coach or mentor. Someone who can give you advice, check your decision making and work closely with you to challenge the business direction and your leadership. A person who partners with you, is onboard with your vision and believes in your ability to execute.

While you may get a mentor or coach such as myself, you could alternatively source a mentor from within your immediate community. I'm talking about people who have been successful in your industry and are now retired or semi-retired. These people have a wealth of wisdom and generally come with great empathy for the challenges you face, having walked in your shoes. Probus clubs, Rotary clubs and community organisations such as men's sheds, and their female equivalents, can be great sources of mentors who would like nothing else than to work with you in designing your future breakthrough business.

The third means to combat the loneliness at the top factor may seem somewhat counterintuitive, but I have found it to be incredibly powerful on the journey. I suggest you join a board or business-style committee, where you will learn a broad range of business practices and skills from likeminded individuals that you can apply to your business model. Hang on, I hear you scream, 'I don't have enough hours in the day now!' Well, they say if you want a job done give it to a busy person. When we live in service, we gain broader perspective. There is an abundance of research that says that when we are in service to others, it has an incredible impact on our sense of wellbeing and confidence.

Most entrepreneurs are busy! Those who are not overwhelmed and chaotic, and my experience is that they are in the minority, prioritise truly important tasks over those unimportant ones that manage to fill our endless to-do lists. They align their priorities with the strategic framework determined by their game plan to create their business by design. They resist being dictated to by other people's demands if those demands don't align with that game plan. We are all busy, but it is through prioritising what is important – those things that Stephen Covey referred to as big rocks – over what is urgent and unimportant that we can find enough time to do what is meaningful and impactful.

Do the work

We are in real danger when we leap into the unknown without doing the work or creating the disciplines that underpin a clear vision for the future model. Adopting a breakthrough attitude must involve an understanding that doing the right work, often unnatural work, is critical to success.

Matt Church is an author, keynote speaker and entrepreneur, who is fond of saying that action brings clarity. This has absolutely been my experience; however, the action he refers to is not blindly letting go of the known without first taking the time and space to plot the path forward. Doing the work means taking the time to get very clear on what your future business by design looks like. By designing your future, you will turn the invisible into the visible, and once the future is seen it can be pursued.

> *The work that, for many, is uncomfortable, beyond their technical skill and personally challenging, is precisely the work that, if genuinely undertaken, can result in a business by design and a different future.*

A business where balance is real and scalability is possible. Changing the way you do things that you have been doing for a long time may feel unpleasant, daunting and risky. Despite this, if you agree that the status quo is no longer acceptable and life wedged under the entrepreneurial ceiling is not much of a life, you can create a breakthrough mindset that, over time, will be clarified by action.

Change can be confronting. I am sure you can come up with a million reasons why you should do nothing and how doing *something* could go horribly wrong. Yes, you're right; there is certainty in doing nothing, but at what cost? You will never have the rewards and choices that come with the creation of a business by design.

You might be able to fool others, but you can't fool yourself. To adopt a breakthrough attitude requires accountability. It is important that, from the outset, you are honest with yourself. Like not speaking Voldemort's name in the Harry Potter series, unspoken and unrecognised self-truths can leave us rooted to the spot and unable to move forward or backward.

A breakthrough mindset requires radical self-assessment and absolute honesty. We must do the hard and uncomfortable work that brings these self-truths to the surface and enables us to address them. We must hear the divisive internal voices that are holding us back from breakthrough, from change, from our business by design.

It won't just happen. Like Djokovic hitting millions of tennis balls across the net, spending hours in the gym and working relentlessly with his mind coach, in those clutch moments the work will make the difference. You too must do the work, do the practice. It is by committing to a different future, and doing the work that aligns with that future, that we can effect real change.

Shift from the technical to the strategic

Taking action to get out of the daily weeds, committing to think bigger and lifting your eyes to a future vision different from what you have known takes courage and practice. It requires a decision.

Embarking on a journey of this magnitude will present you with many challenges, and most of these challenges will appear when looking in the mirror.

> *Breaking through the entrepreneurial ceiling is the ultimate professional development journey.*

This development involves a dramatic shift from the technical skill set that built the business to a strategic skill set of infinite future outcomes identified by exploring new horizons and identifying new opportunities to align to your future aspiration.

Moving from being a technical business owner to a managerial business owner is not only a change of role, but also an exploration of your personal values. For many, your self-worth is tightly entangled with your technical ability. Your skills, honed over a lifetime, say you are good at what you do and this is valued. It validates and confirms who you are and what you do. For many, this is a new frontier and will require self-development, accountability in new disciplines and the parking of ego. For many this will be highly uncomfortable.

For others not so much. They will thrive on the evolution, revel in their newfound knowledge, and willingly let go and enter a new world that is exhilarating, challenging and inspirational. Whatever meaning you attach to the future and whatever values these meanings challenge, the good news is that your world will change. No longer will the grind and chaos look the same every day. Each step forward, and even the odd step back, will have new purpose and meaning. You will look through a strategic lens for challenges to solve, with your eyes firmly fixed on the future business you have designed.

Once you have made the shift from valuing yourself as the technician to valuing yourself in your future strategic state, you have cleared the biggest blocker to commencing the journey. Going from thinking of yourself in the technical sense to thinking of yourself in a managerial, strategic sense is simple, but not easy. You must make the decision to see yourself in a different light, from a different angle, through a different lens.

In looking back over the hundreds of businesses I have worked with, what is clear is that there is no one-size-fits-all. Each owner's business aspiration is as unique as a fingerprint. However, while the individual vision and economic scale of the aspiration may differ, the very personal journey out of chaotic overwhelm towards scalability is similar.

For example, an electrician who dreams of having three teams of sparkies, so he can move off the tools to manage and feed the business, has to make the same momentous decision that an electrician who dreams of hitting $100 million in revenue and securing massive government projects has to make.

These are real-life examples from my clients. I had the privilege of front row seats to the ongoing evolution of both these clients, and many more like them. I witnessed their personal growth, how they wrestled with and overcame self-doubt, imposter syndrome and uncertainty. Each has had to overcome unique struggles and challenges. I would say that once the decision is truly made, the strategic self is valued as much as the technical self and the entrepreneur has committed to the new path, the likelihood of succeeding is strong. They have done the work, they have made the mental shift and they are executing.

When I look back and review client's strategic plans which I had crafted years earlier, it always amazes me from concept to design through to implementation, it always amazes me how many achieve their goals despite the progression from today to tomorrow being far from linear. In the day to day, it can often feel like two steps forward and one step back but, over time, progression is made as long as you stay on the path.

Get gritty

Victor Frankl's 1946 book, *Man's Search for Meaning*, is a compelling read. Frankl was an Austrian Jew who was imprisoned in four Nazi concentration camps during World War II. After the war he studied neurology and psychology and became a professor at the University of Vienna. He went on to develop a treatment program called Logotherapy, which describes a search for meaning in life. He died in Vienna in 1997.

The odds of survival in concentration camps were stacked against you. Only one person in twenty-six came out alive. In his book, Frankl clearly outlines the role optimism plays in survival in such horrendous circumstances. The key to survival, Frankl found, was to identify a purpose in life to feel positive about and immerse yourself in that imagery. Something as simple as picturing opening the door of your home could help you do what was necessary to stay alive. Frankl noted that once prisoners lost hope, they had little chance of survival. In the camps the currency used to barter for meagre rations from the guards and other prisoners was cigarettes. Frankl knew when a man had given up hope; he smoked his cigarettes.

In 2001, Jim Collins and a team of researchers wrote a book called *Good to Great: Why Some Companies Make the Leap and Others Don't*. The team studied S&P 500 Companies and identified five traits successful companies had that contributed to becoming great. The third trait identified was 'confront the brutal facts', and Collins developed the Stockdale Paradox to help explain it.

To take your company from good to great, Collins declared, 'You must maintain unwavering faith that you can and will prevail in the end, regardless of the difficulties, AND at the same time have the discipline to confront the most brutal facts of your current reality, whatever they might be.'

The Stockdale Paradox is named after Admiral Jim Stockdale, who was the highest-ranking officer imprisoned in the notorious prisoner of war camp in Hanoi during the Vietnam War. While imprisoned, Stockdale dedicated himself to improving the well-being of his fellow prisoners. He created an internal tapping language so that prisoners could communicate during periods of enforced silence; he created a system to help prisons work through horrendous torture sessions; and he endlessly negotiated with his Vietnamese captors to support fellow prisoners in the camp. Upon his release Stockdale was awarded the Congressional Medal of Honour in recognition of his bravery. After the war he went on to study psychology at Stanford University.

When Stockdale was asked how he survived the brutality of the concentration camp for such a long time, he responded, 'I never lost faith in the end story. I never doubted not only that I would get out, but also that I would prevail in the end and turn the experience into the defining event in my life, which in retrospect I would not trade.' When asked who didn't make it out, he answered, 'The optimists.' This appears to contradict what he said earlier, but he then goes on to explain that what he meant by optimists were those who set themselves a deadline to be released, such as Easter, Christmas or Thanksgiving. When those dates came and went, like Frankl's men who smoked their cigarettes, these men died of 'a broken heart'. Stockdale's message was that you must never confuse faith that you will prevail with the discipline to confront the brutal facts of your reality, whatever that might be.

Two generations after Stockdale and nearly three generations after Frankl, came Angela Duckworth's 2017 bestselling book *Grit: Why Passion and Resilience are the Secrets to Success*. Duckworth is also a psychologist and professor at the University of Pennsylvania. The Cambridge Dictionary defines grit as: 'Courage and determination despite difficulty'. In dictionary.com it's defined as: 'Firmness of Character; indomitable spirit; pluck'

A key finding of Duckworth's book is that grit trumps talent in predicting success. Further, a key element of sustaining grit is exploring, committing to and connecting with your passion. Connecting with your passion and setting long-term goals can provide the impetus to stay the path and continue the journey, even when things got tough. Duckworth found that grit has two components: passion and perseverance. It is about, 'Working on something you care so much about that you're willing to stay loyal to it.'

Whether you call it grit, optimism or passion, Frankl, Stockdale and Duckworth demonstrate that having a long-term view while confronting the brutal facts in front of us is critical for ultimate success. It is fallacy to think that you can plan for unforeseen events; however, if you can ride the short-term bumps and set about targeting your biggest aspirations in the moments when challenge arises, you are equipped with many of the processes that will help you create a business by design.

Shift the narrative

The stories that we tell ourselves play a pivotal role in how we act, and drive many of our behaviours. If we are to change the way we do things and align our behaviours with a breakthrough game plan, we must change the way we talk to ourselves. Our brain is hardwired for survival, and thousands of years ago this was extremely useful for identifying things that may kill us. But these tendencies are not so useful in the environment of 21st century business.

There is any number of ways you could convince yourself that the current state, as bad as it is, is better than the unknown, but let's look at my top three. Yours may be different or a variation of these, but when I listen to my clients talk about fighting the journey, these are the most common expressions.

You may say to yourself, 'I can't move forward as I don't have a clear plan that I can truly believe in that outweighs the perceived risks.' Let's complete that sentence. 'Oh, and by the way, if I'm honest, I haven't really done the work that could produce this.'

Here's another common statement that potentially roots us to the spot: 'I am not good enough to build this new business model, and I will be exposed as an imposter.' At some point, many of us will suffer from imposter syndrome. It's normal. Acknowledge it, identify evidence to suggest that you *can* in fact do the thing you're telling yourself you can't do, and move on. This is another one of those skills that will get better with practice.

The third statement I often hear, especially when things are feeling out of control is: 'I can't do this, it's all too hard.' This one is more challenging, and requires you to put a gap between the overwhelm and the circumstances. Go for a walk, take a break and get a coffee. Take some time out.

To shift, we first must truly admit to ourselves that the status quo that is our business and our life must change. In order to create the idea in our own mind that this is no longer acceptable, we must associate significant pain and unrewarded sacrifice with our current circumstances – and for many of us this isn't a big stretch. We must admit to ourselves that our current circumstances are not where we need or want to be, and we must believe, develop and practise self-talk that aligns with this view.

Why is this important? We don't have to look very far to see how effective this can be in making genuine change. Alcoholics Anonymous (AA) has a famous twelve-step program that helps people become sober, and the first step is to admit that alcohol controls your life and your life as it is has become unmanageable.

I am not implying that you are an alcoholic, but the feeling of overwhelm and the concept of the business controlling your life may sound familiar. AA calls this breaking the cycle of denial. Giving up the illusion of power and the idea that you have things under control. Many who have undertaken the program say that the first step in the program is the hardest. It is said that step one is the only step you must do perfectly. When people stumble or relapse, they are considered to have a step one problem.

Admitting powerlessness galvanises you for the rest of the program, but importantly, the process uses storytelling to reinforce the reality of your situation. Standing in front of the group, admitting you have a problem and telling your story is a critical part of the process. Research suggests that telling your story reinforces the reality of a painful past and facilitates honesty. In telling your story, you shift your self-talk from denial to resolve.

Storytelling is powerful. Storytellers know a secret to engaging their listeners that has been adopted with great success by advertisers and marketers. There is a reason many of us spend a significant amount of our spare time watching movies and television. The reason is that we love stories. Stories are in our DNA and have been a key communication tool since man first walked the earth. We developed language about 100,000 years ago, cave paintings about 27,000 years ago, and the first writing appeared about 3,500 years ago. Today, we capture our stories through a myriad of digital platforms. Story has been instrumental in shaping our knowledge as a species and ensuring our survival.

Attach new meaning

Perspective is a funny thing. It is the meaning you attach to things that creates perspective and becomes your reality. Having a bigger, aspirational vision of your future allows your mind to engage with a different story. Allows it to attach a different meaning to circumstances that test your resilience and perseverance. It enables you to break down moments and solve issues one handhold, one foothold at a time, while all the while being clear that it is a necessary part of your journey and not the potentially catastrophic event your ego would like you to believe.

In his book *Breaking the Habit of Being Yourself*, bestselling author Dr Joe Dispenza writes that memorised feelings and emotions limit us to recreate the past. When you are in the middle of an experience, the brain receives external information through the senses and goes about making sense of it. Dr Dispenza says, 'Networks of neurons arrange themselves into specific patterns reflecting the external event.' Once that pattern is processed, the brain releases a cocktail of chemicals that produce an emotion or feeling. This makes you feel differently than you did just a few moments before, and you pay attention to what caused this. He goes on to say,

> 'When you identify the event that caused the change, that event in and of itself is called a memory. Neurologically and chemically, you encode that environmental information into your brain and body. Thus, you can remember experiences better because you recall how they felt at the time they happened – feelings and emotions are a chemical record of past experiences.'

I see a version of this scenario played out often in entrepreneurial businesses. Let's say you own an engineering business that makes widgets. Production is way behind schedule and the customers are starting to make noises about being displeased that their goods are not completed as agreed. Your senior team leader in the workshop comes to you saying that the tradespeople have made an error, and this will further delay the product. It is at this point the neurons align and the story you tell yourself begins.

The brain releases chemicals that create emotions, and you align the story with a memory of being yelled at for being late by a client who then took his lucrative business elsewhere. At this moment you feel anxiety, your heart rate increases and your chest feels heavy, like it has a dumbbell sitting on it. You have trouble breathing. You go away picturing the client's reaction and reliving the memory of it. You have the same emotional reaction just thinking about the event as you did when you first experienced it, and your body believes it is experiencing the same event.

It's time to attach new meaning, build new neural pathways and create an alternative scenario.

Understanding what is happening in your brain and how this affects your body in the moment is an opportunity to shift the meaning of that event for you. It is understanding what is occurring in the moment that will enable you to anchor a different thought pattern and reaction. By simply recognising the emotion, telling yourself a different story and committing to move forward, you can make the leap that will help you break through the entrepreneurial ceiling and plot a new path. To change your physical response to stimuli and circumstances, you must change the meaning you associate with that event in the moment.

Big-picture thinking that you can attach new emotions and feelings to is a powerful tool that will help you arrest unhelpful thoughts as they appear, then re-anchor external stimuli that once may have triggered a negative response. Through shifting the meaning of an event to a positive anchor, you will realign neural pathways, and over time more helpful emotions and feelings arise.

If these new truths are to bite and gain enough momentum to help you break through the entrepreneurial ceiling, you must be prepared to be uncomfortable, recognise the feelings and emotions you are experiencing and create new realities. Sometimes small, but always deliberate actions, supported by the rituals of your new reality, will ultimately see you shift.

Now, back to Novack Djokovic. The story at the start of this chapter ended in 2016. Remarkably, in 2022 at the age of thirty-five, Djokovic is still playing. He has won eighty-five championships, competed in over 1,100 matches, achieved the most Grand Slam singles titles in the modern era and spent the longest time in history (372 weeks) perched on top of the rankings as world number one.

Djokovic has not been without controversy and challenges during that time. In 2017 he had a poor year and sacked his coach, and in 2018 he underwent elbow surgery before returning to the top of his game and the world rankings in 2019. Most recently, in 2022, he was the centre of an international firestorm when he was deported from Australia on the eve of the Australian Open for not complying with Australian COVID vaccination laws.

I am sure these were challenging times for the Serbian great, but in sticking to his process he has had a long and extraordinary career. The lesson from the Djokovic story, which is equally true for your business, is that small, incremental increases in performance predicated on targeted actions can have amazing impact. In Djokovic's case, a six per cent improvement in points won led to a 41% increase in matches won and an extra $13,700,000 per annum. Now that's leverage!

Adopting a breakthrough mindset will provide the foundation to scale your business. It will provide the long-term grit to stay the path. It will help you enjoy the journey in the day to day and not be hanging out for the future when things may get better. In adopting a breakthrough mindset, you will build a rewarding business that can provide you with the day-to-day challenge, enjoyment and sense of purpose and accomplishment that only comes from doing the work, getting uncomfortable and confronting your challenges.

BREAKTHROUGH

BITES

- Going through the entrepreneurial ceiling into a new world requires courage.

- The drive to change must be stronger than the uncertainty that precedes it.

- For the entrepreneur this is a very personal journey, and every person who has taken their business through the ceiling has done so by treading their own path.

- Once you're in the moment, it is generally too late to work through what you should do. You will succumb to the path of least resistance, which is likely to keep you firmly wedged under the entrepreneurial ceiling.

- Nothing worthwhile is easy, and it can take many years to become an overnight sensation.

- It is hard to make significant change on your own, and it can be lonely at the top.

- The real danger occurs when we leap into the unknown without doing the work or creating the disciplines that underpin the clear vision for the future model.

- Adopting a breakthrough attitude must involve an understanding that doing the right work, often unnatural and uncomfortable work, is critical to succeed.

- Breaking through the entrepreneurial ceiling is the ultimate professional development journey.

- Once you have made the shift from valuing yourself as the technician to valuing yourself in your future strategic state, you have cleared the biggest blocker in commencing the journey.

- Connecting with your passion and setting long-term goals can provide the impetus to stay the path and continue, even when things get tough.

- The stories that we tell ourselves play a pivotal role in how we act and drive many of our behaviours.

- Big-picture thinking that you can attach new emotions and feelings to is a powerful tool.

- Adopting a breakthrough mindset will provide the foundation to scale your business.

5

Eliminate Key-Person Risk

A single point of failure

One of the biggest blocks to truly building a business by design is you the entrepreneur, or worse, an employee who could leave any time, being the source of all knowledge in a critical element of your business offering. Key-person risk is a critical consideration in a business valuation for good reason. The more key-person risks the organisation has, the more likely it is that something will go wrong and impact the commercial viability and/or continuity of the business.

Creating a scalable business is about having no individual element or elements of the business totally dependent on one person.

This key-person risk usually centres around the entrepreneur, but may involve a whole range of people with mission-critical roles. Should they leave the business, this will have catastrophic consequences and represent what engineers call a single point of failure.

I recently watched the compelling Netflix documentary *Downfall, the Case Against Boeing*[9]. The documentary outlines the story of how catastrophic a single point of failure can be. On 29 October 2018, Lion Air Flight 610 took off from Jakarta's Soekarno-Hatta International Airport carrying 189 passengers and crew. The plane was a Boeing 737-Max. The 737-Max was new to the market, had larger, more fuel-efficient engines and was in high demand. Airlines around the world looked to invest in the new plane to cut costs. Fuel, of course, is a major cost contributor.

Flight 610's take-off was uneventful. After lifting off, the plane banked steeply and turned 180 degrees, heading out to sea towards its destination. But not long into the climb phase, and with no warning, the instrument panel in the cockpit lit up. All hell broke loose as the audio and visual warnings screamed at the startled pilots and the plane, for no apparent reason, began to dive. The pilots, as they were trained, stayed calm and wrestled the aircraft back to a level altitude, only to have it seemingly 'fight back' and dive back towards the sea again. Tragically, the pilots eventually lost the battle and the plane crashed violently into the sea, killing all 189 passengers and crew on board.

Initially, considering Boeing's overall safety record, the exceptional safety record of 737, which had been flying for over forty years, and the fact that it was a new plane that crashed, it was speculated that pilot error was to blame.

But over the coming days it was discovered that an inbuilt safety system, the MCAS, caused the crash. A plane that is too vertical can stall in mid-air. The MCAS system had been specifically designed for this new model 737, which had the potential to become too vertical due to the weight of the new, significantly bigger engines mounted on a forty-year-old fuselage design.

Tragically, not long into the investigation, it was discovered that pilots flying the new aircraft had not been told about this new system, let alone trained on it. Under intense scrutiny, Boeing quickly rolled out pilot training and Boeing began work on an urgent software fix to resolve the malfunction. The global fleet of Boeing 737-Maxs, of which there were significant numbers at this point, continued flying.

Less than five months later, Ethiopian Airlines Flight 302, again a new Boeing 737-Max, left Addis Ababa Airport bound for Kenya. Not long into the flight, as was the case with the Lion Air Flight, the MCAS system again kicked in despite the plane flying exactly as it should. The pilots this time were better prepared. They had been trained on the system and how to disarm it. The protocols allowed the pilots ten seconds to react, and according to the flight recorder they did so within that. But despite the pilots' best efforts and their training, the plane continued to nosedive, tragically killing the 157 people on board.

Globally, the Boeing 737 Max was grounded and would remain so for the next eighteen months.

So how did this go so tragically wrong ... twice?

It turns out the MCAS system was controlled by a sensor mounted on the left front nose of the plane. The sensor was mounted on a metal object jutting out of the body of the plane and angled at 90 degrees, and collected data on the pitch of the aircraft. This information was then fed back to the MCAS onboard computer. In the investigation that followed, it was determined that the sensor was prone to damage from bird strike, as well as calibration and maintenance issues that could potentially lead to false readings.

Boeing engineers had broken a golden rule of aircraft design, and indeed engineering. They created a system that had a single point of failure. This catastrophic error ultimately led to the deaths of 346 people.

When I look at businesses trapped below the entrepreneurial ceiling, the common theme I see is a single point of failure. Flawed business models where critical business systems and operational imperatives are highly dependent upon you, the entrepreneurial owner. Process and policy in the entrepreneur's head, and nowhere else. This is a single point of failure waiting to happen. Nothing is ever wrong until it is.

Creating business systems that mitigate against a single point of failure is critical for you to break through the entrepreneurial ceiling. While I am sure you get this, there can be many pitfalls in getting this done. Concentrated effort, perseverance, systems thinking, harnessing information technology and capacity-stacking readily available solutions are all key elements in effectively breaking through.

Concentrate your efforts

Consultants are fond of asking, 'How would the business fare if the key person in the business (in this case you, the entrepreneur) were hit by a bus?' Interestingly, my experience has been that most entrepreneurs are more than happy to play the odds that this will never happen. Playing the odds for Boeing, in betting they would have a software fix before there was another incident, tragically didn't work. The truth is, it also rarely works in the long term for an entrepreneurial business.

In most cases, of course, the entrepreneur who bets that nothing will happen to them will be right. They will continue to turn up to work and, while they're fit and energetically at the helm, the business will function. This, however, is flawed thinking and a dangerous gamble. Life under the entrepreneurial ceiling, where you're the single point of contact, the source of all knowledge and the focus of client interaction, is hectic. When you're at capacity there is no room to think, no room to evolve, no ability to do things differently. You are trapped!

In his book *Essentialism, The Disciplined Pursuit of Less*, author Greg McKeown says that when we are highly reactive and there is ongoing demand for our time and energies, it leads to diffused effort. We get spread thinner and thinner, and in the end achieve very little of substance. He states, 'The way of the Essentialist means living by design, not by default. Essentialism is a disciplined, systematic approach for determining where our highest point of contribution lies, then making execution of those things almost effortless.'

Individuals at capacity rarely appear to be executing effortlessly. They generally appear frantic. Working at full bore and red-lining for extended periods of time is unsustainable. Given this, why do you persist and insist on being the source of all knowledge, the single point of failure and the hero in your own show?

Well, to be fair, this single point of failure can creep up on the poor, unsuspecting business owner. Your business is growing, your service or product is in demand and you are reactive to your client needs. They love you and you love them. They respect and admire you for what you offer, and you appreciate their business. A match made in heaven. Until one day, suddenly, the business has significant issues up and down the supply chain, staff are exiting and customers are deserting in droves. The business finds itself weak, under-resourced, dysfunctional and on life support. This situation is likely to be doing untold damage, like a rudderless ship lost at seas drifting through the night. It relies on a single point of failure that is, in effect, broken.

Perseverance pays off

One organisation I mentored has taken a very typical journey through the transition development stage to achieve break-through. This husband and wife business specialises in industrial electrical work. They predominantly service quasi-government water-management organisations, designing and building water-management and electrical infrastructure. This business grew dramatically in the early years, based on the ability to support infrastructure design as well as build and implement that infrastructure downstream (pardon the pun). This compet-itive advantage was further enhanced through the ability to be extremely agile and rapidly respond to client demands when compared with more corporate competitors.

In the early days the company literally ticked through every stage of the entrepreneurial journey, from start-up to high growth and customer driven, then on to chaotic, overwhelmed and at capacity. As the company grew and reacted to customer demands, they found that their projects were becoming more and more remote and harder to manage. This meant significant travel and a lot of learning on the run.

As is the norm in the high growth phase and chaotic phase, there was lots of rework and redesign, and some very unhappy clients who had taken a risk on a less experienced company to save costs. When this occurred, emotions bubbled to the surface. In the mad scramble to resolve whatever was the issue of the day, tensions ran high, often resulting in fiery and unpleasant team interactions. The blame game was in full swing. It became a very unpleasant place to work at times.

As the business grew, the owners continued to pursue bigger and more complex jobs. Often these were won on tender, with the quasi-government body putting the job out to the open market and inviting bids to undertake the works. This business, despite their relative inexperience, often won jobs by undercutting the competition while they built technical and project management expertise.

The key competitive advantage through the growth years, however, was clear. The company was able to support the client by coming up with designs that produced innovation-driven cost savings. This ability to consult, design and construct ultimately laid the foundation for the future growth.

As the projects and workload mounted, it became obvious the entrepreneurial couple was struggling. The strong, energetic entrepreneurial leader became the central figure in daily operations, and all decision making and technical support went through him. This unsustainable model saw the leader under significant pressure all day every day, and was a cause of immense frustration for the team around him.

Further, they were dealing with quasi-government organisations that live and breathe structure. An entrepreneurial organisation that managerially is somewhat loose, that relies on a key individual to manage operational outcomes and solve all problems clearly would not, and did not work in this highly structured, policy-driven world. Quasi-government organisations are extremely risk averse. To work effectively with them requires detailed compliance systems and capabilities. They require quality management processes that mitigate risk. This business had not yet developed this level of sophistication. The owners knew something had to change, but where to start?

To align the client's needs with what the organisation needed, and capture the intellectual property and operating systems that resided in the owner's head, it was necessary to start with two things:

1. Operating manuals that clearly set out how to do things; and
2. The technical infrastructure (hardware and software) to utilise these quality manuals in the field and provide evidence to the client that process had been followed.

When it became obvious that the business could not grow without these in place, the owners went to the first place most people would go – the internet. They found a templated quality manual, and went about trying to make it relevant to their organisation. After months of working through this tedious process, burning resources and copious amounts of time, and frustratingly still not achieving what they wanted, they realised the task was too big. Further, they genuinely began to understand the value of such a process.

Take two. The owners shifted to the second phase and found an expert in writing legislative and policy documents. This expert set about the task of taking what had already been done internally and turning it into a usable document – one that would satisfy clients' legal requirements, and also provide the ability to participate in bigger tenders. After three months of going backwards and forwards, it became clear that the expert did not have enough industry knowledge to draft satisfactory policies, so they parted ways.

The third attempt to create the system involved significantly more cost and included a recognised accreditation and audit process. The company brought in a specialist consultant to create an information management system (IMS). This is a trilogy of manuals consisting of a quality manual, safety manual and environmental manual. These would be specifically tailored to the client and would be recognised by government authorities. Aside from ongoing project compliance, these would pave the way to participate in much more significant tenders and projects and, most importantly, do so as the lead organisation and not a subcontractor.

The company decided to not only follow this path, but to embrace the process and live it across the organisation. They vowed to do things differently. The major shift that this business made was to recognise that properly constructed, professional documentation was an expertise they needed to source externally, and a key transitional element of their breakthrough and structured growth. Having built the business on rapid-fire responsiveness, the entrepreneur had to learn to exercise a greater degree of patience and take a longer view, as the documentation and audit completion process took approximately twelve months.

The fourth phase in the process was to shift the internal culture of the organisation to value the documentation and the process, and create internal checks and balances to ensure the documents were completed. Traditionally the business had flown by the seat of its pants, at times making up the rules as they went along and always relying on the entrepreneur. The evolution towards a scalable business model continues today, but with one of the owners driving the process and championing its importance, the business has achieved the compliance level that now works for both them and the quasi-government clients they service. This has laid the foundation for a consistent, quality driven, scalable business.

Working in this way could not have been more foreign to this entrepreneurial business, and the organisation struggled to make the genuine shift from utilising their technical, trade-based expertise to moving to an accountable, structured and documented business system. But they persevered. Some employees, who were used to doing things their own way, left the organisation, while others, who had come from more structured organisations, brought their expertise to the business. This further accelerated the growth into a more family-corporate style of business that relied on processes, business systems and quality management, rather than an entrepreneurial owner who had the potential to be a single point of failure.

This case study is this client's journey, and only one example of how to build a business structure to break through the entrepreneurial ceiling. The common theme in the transition phase to breakthrough is to develop capability away from key people in the organisation and capture process and policy in the business system.

Systems thinking

It is a significant and deliberate shift for the entrepreneurial business to move from creating products and services that rely upon individual knowledge and the verbal handing down of information to a documented, structured business system. A system that enables repetition of process and fosters quality management. Interestingly, as we saw in the case study earlier in this chapter, it is at this point in the entrepreneurial journey that external support and expertise can have the most impact. The laborious work of documenting and cataloguing is often very foreign to the entrepreneur, and historically it is work that they have not valued compared with tasks that are technical and highly operational.

This is a critical crossroad in the entrepreneurial journey that, if not done effectively, could hinder the growth of an organisation for years. It is...

> *A sliding doors moment when the road less travelled, although it may seem longer, will ultimately be the shortest route.*

The concept of systems thinking was first introduced to me through Michael Gerber's famous book on building business systems in SMEs, *The E-Myth Revisited, Why Most Small Businesses Don't Work and What to Do About It*. This book was rewritten from his original works in 1995. It has subsequently sat at the top of the *New York Times* bestseller list for over three decades – and for good reason.

In his book, Gerber walks the reader through several small business case studies where entrepreneurs have been able to create repeatable, scalable operating processes and procedures that have freed them to grow their businesses or do work inside their businesses that they truly love. This process has been life changing for millions of business owners and inspired thousands of consulting practices around the world to follow the Gerber methodology.

Gerber famously said the test of whether you have a small business, or a job, is, if you have a small business, you should be able to pick up the phone, ring work and say, 'Hi its me, see you in six months.'

As a young consultant I got my first big break through a Victorian State Government program called Business Continuity. The program was created in 2006 to address the devastating impacts a ten-year drought was having on small businesses in regional communities. The idea was that I would meet with a business, we would undertake a SWOT (strengths, weaknesses, opportunities, threats) analysis, and have a conversation about where the business was at and where it needed to go. I would then go away, review their financials, document the conversation, and come back with a road map and implementation plan that the business could enact to help generate cashflow and stimulate economic activity.

The initial program ran in a small north-eastern Victorian town called Mansfield, which was a tourist mecca with a 53% non-resident base. Much of the summer tourism depended on the sizeable lake on the outskirts of the town. Due to extreme drought the lake was down to less than 15% capacity, making it unsuitable for boating or fishing. Without the tourist dollars many businesses were suffering. Those that were geared towards tourism were doing it particularly hard.

The local council signed up ten businesses to undertake the program, and I was away. The funds assigned to each business were minimal, so the program had to be delivered very efficiently and at times it felt like speed dating. The town was about an hour and a half from my office, so I had to make the most of every trip and visited three or four clients, for a couple of hours per client, each day.

The clients I visited began to see some success and economic activity, so the council invited ten more businesses to join the program. Then Wangaratta Shire and Moira Shire in the state's north-east also joined the program. Each region had specific issues and unique circumstances. By the end of 2007, I had met with and delivered 107 individual action and implementation plans. It was a crash course in consulting, and I was exhausted by the end of this period, but I had met with so many small business owners across the region that I felt I had a really good handle on the challenges facing small regional businesses and a solid understanding of the issues facing the entrepreneurs who ran them.

So, what were my biggest learnings from this extraordinarily intense project?

I learned that Michael Gerber was right. Most small business owners operate like they have a job, not a business. Many worked for less than the minimum wage, electing to pay suppliers, landlords and banks ahead of themselves. Most worked extraordinarily long hours and were passionate and dedicated. Some were emotionally drained and mentally 'over' their business. They were often trapped in a vicious cashflow cycle, in too much debt to exit the business so they could get a real job, but barely making enough money to pay the bills. They were physically, emotionally and financially on the edge. Many were living on borrowed funds propped up by equity loans against their homes, which they continued to draw down on to survive. If this was a snap shot of the typical Australian small business, then many were doing it hard.

The thing that really struck me, however, was the fact that although most of these people were hard working and dedicated, the work they valued most were the tasks that physically serviced their customers. Few spent much time or gave much thought to working *on* their business as well as *in* it. Most acted like they had a job, were consumed with the operational tasks, and rarely examined why they did what they did or how they could do it differently. This aligns with Gerber's view of why most small businesses fail, and I saw it on the ground firsthand. I had an amazing number of conversations that went along the lines of:

Me: 'What differentiates you from your competitors?'

Owner: 'Our quality and service.'

Me: 'Oh, that's great, tell me about that.'

They would then tell me about how wonderful their service was. How they went above and beyond for their customers and how their customers kept coming back as a result.

Me: 'Fantastic, can you please go and get your quality manual so I can have a look at how you deliver on your quality consistently, day in and day out.'

Owner: 'Oh no we don't have one of those!'

Me: 'Really, I'd have thought if that's your point of difference and the major reason your customers choose your business over your competitors, then you would have protected that by documenting how you do it, ensuring you and your staff can replicate it time and time again.'

Owner: 'Nope!'

This too was Michael Gerber's point. If you don't take the time to capture your point of difference in a documented system of 'how we do things around here', it is unlikely that your competitive advantage can be sustained and highly unlikely that it can be replicated. It is only by working on the business and capturing our competitive advantage in a business system that enables easy access to key information that we can create consistent outcomes and client experiences. This process builds capacity in our businesses, and is a catalyst to breaking through the entrepreneurial ceiling.

The world has changed considerably since Gerber wrote his book in 1995. Smartphones, the internet and cloud-based subscription models have given the entrepreneur new and wonderous tools to capture their operating systems more elegantly and efficiently than the clunky, time-consuming operations manual.

David Jenyns was a student of Michael Gerber's, and his 2020 book, *Systemology*, applies Gerber's principles to a modern world and modern technology. Jenyns outlines a seven-step process that uses tools such as video to capture information, while leveraging the whole team to create the business system. The outcome of Jenyns' system is a searchable library of operating procedures that ensure the intellectual property of the business and its key people are captured within the business system. It harnesses the power of modern and rapidly evolving software and hardware technologies to help drive, capture and promote productivity while reducing errors and creating the business systems that facilitate entrepreneurial breakthrough. While the methodology is different, the message is the same.

Without working on the business and carving out time to create a recorded business system, you are likely to have significant key-person risk and a single point of failure, and are unlikely to break through the entrepreneurial ceiling.

You will be doomed to porpoise in a world of chaos and

overwhelm, reliant on shifts of personal energy to move the business forward and maintain momentum. Eventually the energy tank will run dry, you will run out of steam and the cycle will commence its downward spiral.

The secret to documenting and recording a business system that allows you to transition through the entrepreneurial ceiling is to identify those processes that have the biggest impact on how the business operates and the most reliance on the entrepreneur. Allocate periods to focus on these big rocks and, one by one, create the systems that will build capacity and develop the business and its people.

Building systems one on top of the other (stacking) will create a library of intellectual property your people can use to understand key tasks. This will build fundamental capabilities that will, over time, free you, the business owner, from many of the daily operations and enable you to one day pick up the phone and say, 'Hi it's me … see you in six months.'

Smart work

Productivity expert and author of the book *Smart Work*, Dermot Crowley, discovered that many entrepreneurs are drowning in urgent email and other people's priorities. These things get in the way of what is truly important in a business. According to Crowley, we are not leveraging the tools at our fingertips enough. Even though we use tools such as smartphones and email every day, we have not fully harnessed their power. In fact, Crowley believes that the average worker uses about 20% of the functionality contained in a tool such as Microsoft's Outlook, even though it often consumes a large portion of their working day. This makes no sense. It feels like the classic Covey 'sharpen the saw' issue, where we are too busy chopping down the metaphorical tree to sharpen the axe.

Crowley believes that we are using the tools and strategies of the analogue world of pen and paper, and applying this thinking to digital productivity tools. This is compounded by the nature of the communication mediums we now use, which demand immediate action and response. So, what's Crowley's answer and how might we apply this in a modern business environment, where we want to create continuous improvement as we move from chaotic to scalable?

He puts forward a three-pronged approach.

1. Centralise our inputs into one organising tool;
2. Organise our inputs to separate the noise from the important work; and
3. Understand our outputs by clearly defining and living our productivity goals in the day to day.

I only have to look at how I have managed to scale my own practice to see how stacking IT solutions can have real productivity gains. I have cobbled together a combination of products that provide incredible efficiencies in my world. With cheap, readily available apps and cloud-based IT platforms, you can design an IT ecosystem where each element forms a symbiotic relationship with another.

This has produced a whole new way of thinking and working with IT. Gone are the days when we had to choose a one-size-fits-all solution that did some things really well, some things adequately and other things poorly.

SMEs have never had greater access to extraordinary computing and software systems than we have today. The major shift that plays into the SME's hands is the move to cloud-based subscription models. A rent rather than buy model, which enables great flexibility and ensures products are kept up to date and evolve over time.

We don't always get it right the first time. I took several missteps in looking for an IT coaching platform that could capture all my client engagements in one place and build capability as I grew the business. The good news is that, under a subscription model, the financial damage is minimal. I have finally settled on several products that talk to each other and provide very powerful efficiencies. Game changer!

As I think it through, it dawns on me how important it has been for so many of my entrepreneurial business owners, who have achieved breakthrough and now have businesses by design, to have stacked their IT programs and used them as an enabler to create robust and sustainable business systems.

It's not just IT platforms that can bring about significant change in how entrepreneurial businesses operate and mitigate single points of failure. Robotic technology is just starting to truly infiltrate the manufacturing workspace. Laser-cutting machines, welding robots, paint robots and materials-handling robots are becoming more affordable and smarter. Today's BMW is tomorrow's Hyundai. No longer are these machines solely in the realm of big business. They are now becoming accessible to the SME.

Stacking your technology and capability one piece at a time, in both software and hardware will, over time, pull cost out of producing goods and services.

It will act as an enabler for SMEs to play in new and dynamic industries that have traditionally been the domain of big business, as well as create productivity gains previously out of reach. Advances in affordable technology, a shift to a cloud-based rental model for complex software and a reduction in the cost of hardware, along with improved internet access, speed and reliability, means that IT and technology stacking has never been more accessible to the entrepreneurial business owner. It should be a key resource to support systems-driven business and mitigate against key-person risk.

It is very common for an entrepreneur to be the single point of failure, with many of the business systems firmly entrenched between your ears and not documented. This is one of the key barriers to breaking through the entrepreneurial ceiling. IT systems in a modern business play a pivotal role in accelerating business growth and help capture business rules and systems. However, they should not be used as business system creators. It pays to start with the end in mind and do the work to create the system before identifying IT platforms that align with what you're looking to achieve. This is better than squeezing your operational processes into an inflexible IT solution. There are plenty of war stories of how this has come unstuck, and I am sure you will have your own.

SMEs now have access to tools formerly only available to big businesses. It is setting up business systems and playing like a big business that will help you break through the entrepreneurial ceiling and scale your business. One day you might just find that you have become a big business yourself.

Back to our industrial electricians. Today the business has

doubled in size since it captured its IMS. It is a major player in water infrastructure design and construction. It has built its reputational resources and is well regarded in the market. Most importantly, the business today does not rely operationally on its owners. They have broken through the entrepreneurial ceiling. One has branched out into creating business systems for other businesses, a field she feels passionate about, and she loves being in service. The other continues to pursue bigger and better jobs, playing very much an ambassadorial role in the company as the business continues to evolve.

There is still work to do, but they have transitioned through the entrepreneurial ceiling and today are well on their way to creating a business by design and a family-corporate business model that is rewarding and scalable.

BREAKTHROUGH
BITES

- One of the biggest blockers to truly building a business by design is that you the entrepreneur, or worse still, an employee who is the source of all knowledge, could leave any time.

- Creating a scalable business is about having no individual element or elements of the business dependent on one person.

- In my experience, most entrepreneurs are content playing the odds that nothing will happen to them.

- The key elements in the transition phase to breakthrough are to develop capability away from the key people in the organisation and capture process and policy in the business system.

- The laborious work of documenting and cataloguing is often very foreign to the entrepreneur, and historically it is work that they have not valued when compared with technical and highly operational tasks.

- Without working on the business and carving out time to create a recorded business system, you are likely to have significant key-person risk and a single point of failure, and unlikely to break through the entrepreneurial ceiling.

- The secret to documenting and recording a business system that allows you to transition through the entrepreneurial system is to identify those processes that have the biggest impact on how the business operates and rely most on the entrepreneur.

- SMEs have never had greater access to extraordinary computing and software systems than they have today.

- Stacking your technology and capability one piece at a time, in both software and hardware, will, over time, pull cost out of producing goods and services.

6

Rethink and Grow Your Team

Build your organisational capacity

n 2008 the global financial crisis hit, starting with subprime mortgage lenders in the United States and sending economic ripples across the globe like a stone thrown into a pond. In Australia, we were insulated from the full impact. To ensure the economy did not dip into recession like many other countries around the world, the Federal Government created several community infrastructure projects. These included the building and upgrading of school and community halls, as well as a subsidised scheme that provided grant funding for domestic homeowners to install insulation in their ceilings to reduce energy consumption. These projects were hastily rolled out to stimulate the economy quickly.

At this time, I had completed the strategic plan for a small, but rapidly growing structural steel company in a medium-sized regional town and was advising on its implementation.

The structural steel market was highly competitive, with many local and regional players. These companies constructed and rigged commercial buildings, and would benefit the most from the coming projects to upgrade school and community halls. These companies ramped up in haste. More people, higher wages, bigger premises and offices, higher margins, higher pricing and more equipment. Wage inflation took off as companies fought for skilled tradespeople to meet demand. The escalation was amazing to watch as new school and community halls began to pop up everywhere.

Coincidentally, I volunteered on my children's school board, and we were also the beneficiary of a nice, shiny new hall, so I got to see it from both sides.

By 2010 many of the projects had been completed, and the work dried up. Structural steel companies that were now geared to do a much bigger revenue number that, in the aftermath of the government stimulation, did not exist, found themselves over resourced. They had too many top end expensive managers, wages that were now unsustainable, redundant equipment lying around, expensive offices that were no longer needed – and not enough work. Like pigs at a feedlot, they had stuck their snouts in the proverbial trough, and now the food had run out and they were starving.

Future projects had been brought forward from the natural cycle of infrastructure spend to capitalise on the government funding, but once this tap was turned off, a vacuum was created. Many companies panicked, and in the months that followed there was a significant correction. Initially there were redundancies everywhere, and several businesses folded. Others reinvented themselves and left the industry.

Right from the outset of the government stimulus, my client went about it differently. They used the glut of funds pouring in to enhance their business. They invested in lean programs to become more efficient. They implemented quality systems to ensure their standards were first rate. They created a cadet academy, and instead of participating in an escalating wage war to get talent, they fostered a culture of inclusion and trained and apprenticed new tradespeople in what was a very dynamic and exciting environment. It didn't end there. They invested in amplifying their point of difference, which enabled them to capture more elements of the build. They diversified and brought on plumbers, which enabled them to do elements of the build downstream that other companies outsourced, such as roofing and cladding. They moved upstream of structural steel fabrication and invested in developing engineering capability, automation and high-end project management skills, all the while learning, growing and becoming more efficient in developing their business systems and processes.

When the government spending party ended and the music stopped, my client owned more of the supply chain. They had created a business that had the right mix of top end skills and workshop and supply chain efficiencies, and a clear competitive advantage. This meant they could now compete with the best in the business. The infrastructure market did not dry up completely, but there was scarcity and the market was highly competitive and price conscious. The ability to do more work inhouse enabled the company to pull costs out of a project and gave them a cost advantage in the market. Their regional base had overhead advantages, and they had a raft of skilled tradespeople they had nurtured and grown. They appealed to prospective suitors because they were a great story, were cost competitive, produced quality outcomes and were easy to deal with.

Their strategy and aspirations were clear and defined. They knew where they wanted to be and had developed a strategic plan to get there. They built a strong, resilient culture of quality and excellence. They took the hard road to long-term success rather than the short, easy road, and everyone in the organisation understood this. Their culture was one of quality, eye for detail and no shortcuts, with constant collaboration to ensure everyone knew they belonged. The people in this business had the unwavering belief that the leadership team had the ball. Humble, inclusive and determined, this leadership team knew where they were headed.

As a side note, Australia's current infrastructure boom – on the back of the COVID pandemic – feels similar in many respects, and the lessons from the GFC are relevant today.

This story demonstrates the value of treading your own path and not getting caught up in the short-lived fear of missing out and the hype of the day, but rather lifting your eyes to a sustainable future and investing heavily in that future when the environment is ripe to do so. It is not often that we as business owners can recognise boom or bust times when we're in them. Rather, it is after the fact that we see these periods for what they are.

One of the most successful investors in history, Warren Buffet, says that it is too difficult to try to predict the market, so what he does is explore businesses he understands, look for favourable conditions and invests accordingly. Like Buffet's investment strategies, setting your own strategic direction, assembling your team in accordance with that direction, and seeking a competitive advantage, rather than trying to predict the market, is critical for long-term success.

As a breakthrough business owner looking to build a business you design, it is essential that you rethink the organisational structure of your business and align it with your strategic direction.

A team that is unbalanced, either in too much expensive experience or too little experience, will spend much of the day managing cashflow or firefighting problems. A balanced team, with the capability to achieve the aspiration of the business, well-defined career paths for individuals, and the internal capability to meet client demands, has many of the resources needed to break through the entrepreneurial ceiling and build a scalable and rewarding business model.

To build a great team, you must lead a quest. You must leverage your knowledge, inspire confidence and challenge groupthink. Get these elements of rethinking and growing your team right, and you will accelerate your business and personal growth, have confidence in your direction, stimulate a great team and create a wonderful business that people will want to be part of.

Achieve this and you will inspire others to help you do the heavy lifting of building business systems, managing people, wowing customers and, brick by brick, building your business by design. Your people will be suited to the roles they play. They will have clarity on what success looks like for them and they will likely thrive in this new environment. Your progression will accelerate as new people with new experience bring in new ways of thinking.

You may be reading this thinking it's about nurturing others and doing more of the people stuff that you don't really enjoy. To some extent this is true, but the real beneficiary of building a winning team is you. You will build capacity across the organisation aligned with your aspiration, but above all, you will have the freedom to do the work you love the way you want and play to the strengths you have.

For thousands of years, mankind has congregated in groups and worked together to better the tribe, with individuals playing to their strengths to harness their collective skill for the good of the community. In doing so, we have become the most successful species on Earth. Creating your tribe to harness the collective good is a critical element of moving on from chaos and overwhelm and accelerating progression through the entrepreneurial ceiling towards scalability and reward.

Lead a quest

In his bestselling book, *How to Lead a Quest*, Dr Jason Fox says, 'As soon as we step outside the relentless busy work, we begin to realise and appreciate that our current (default) business model and modus operandi may not be relevant in future contexts.' As discussed, if we are to break through the entrepreneurial ceiling, we must recognise that what got us to today will not get us to tomorrow.

Our future direction requires a new game plan, one that inspires us, motivates us, gets us out of the daily weeds and, above all, interests us. There is no point designing a game plan and future business state that does not align with that which floats our boat!

Having said that:

> *It's not enough that our quest provides us with purpose; it must inspire our people as well.*

You will be calling on them to march side by side with you on your quest to scalability, and if you genuinely expect them to do this, the least you can do is create a culture and role that works for them.

Many overcomplicate this process, but the reality is that it doesn't have to be that hard. The *process* you adopt in developing the direction to achieve your business by design is just as important as the direction itself. If we harness the collective wisdom of the group in developing our quest, they will be more invested. On this quest, we are looking for leaders and foot soldiers who believe in what we are doing and willingly provide discretionary effort on behalf of the team. To achieve this, you must create opportunities to collaborate and communicate with the organisation and talk to the vision in the day to day. You must never take for granted that you have successfully communicated the direction the company is going, and what success will look like.

> *It is critical that everyone understands their role and value in achieving the collective good.*

You must seize opportunities to celebrate wins and highlight effort. You must take the time to celebrate the individual and showcase what good performance looks like. You must ensure your people have the resources they need and the practical skills required to undertake the tasks you give them. Above all, you must enjoy the journey. Have fun focusing on the day-to-day activities that align with your quest and encourage others to do the same.

Dr Fox said, 'Pioneering leadership must start (continue and flourish) with someone and that someone may well be you.' You set the tone. You communicate the vision. You inspire the troops. When things get difficult and your people are in the weeds, it is you who must lift their eyes to a bigger picture and provide the perspective that drives discretionary effort, purpose and belonging.

How are you bringing your tribe along in creating a quest that enables them to see a future direction where they belong and have the means to contribute effectively in a meaningful way?

Leverage your knowledge

As stated earlier, mankind has been extremely successful in harnessing individual talents to maximise the impact of the group. Focusing on building the capabilities of others has facilitated the transfer of knowledge, maximised the likelihood of success and removed operational dependency on an individual to be good at all tasks.

In the modern business environment, these fundamental survival traits have great relevance in how we build successful businesses by design. The most fundamental of entrepreneurial issues that keeps a business below the ceiling and stops breakthrough is, invariably, you the entrepreneur.

Believing that no one can do it like you creates a knowledge and operational bottleneck. This means the business depends on your technical knowledge and operational input to function. The stage that you, the business owner, are at in the porpoising cycle will inevitably dictate business performance.

It is interesting how this journey often evolves. Even with a clear vision of the future, you are often reluctant to let go of the control and processes that you have created. It is only by focusing on building capability in others that the transition phase can succeed.

I am sure you will agree that while the theory of building capacity and capability in others is sound, it is very difficult to do in the day to day. It requires dedicated effort, a willingness to let go and faith that your tribe has the ball. This can be challenging. Learning to let go when your personal reputation and client relationships are at stake can take time. Having said that, let go you must. Delegation is critical if you are to have the business you desire and make the shift from daily chaos and overwhelm to a business by design.

> *The key ingredient that supports the shift in you is confidence; however, the paradox you face is that you can't become confident without letting go!*

Confidence in your people, confidence in your systems, confidence in your product. The reality is that this will take time and there will be mistakes. In the early stages of leveraging your knowledge into others and releasing the reins, you will often find yourself 'fixing' issues. Issues with responsiveness, issues with quality, issues with clients. Ongoing issues where others do things differently from you. But don't fool yourself. It's not just others who require development, so do you! If I'm walking past the dog obedience school on a Sunday morning and see a Labrador not sitting for its owner, I am not looking at the Labrador;

I'm looking at the owner.

To move through the entrepreneurial ceiling and get out of the weeds, you will need to effectively leverage the knowledge you have acquired and developed often over many years. This does not happen overnight; the skills of effective management and communication must be learned and practised. This can be uncomfortable; in fact, it *must* get uncomfortable for you to know that you are undergoing true transformation. If you are not uncomfortable, you are not evolving.

Simon Sinek is an inspirational speaker and the author of many books, including *Leaders Eat Last*. In this book, Sinek talks about how great leaders inspire action in others by focusing on the development of the person in their charge over everything else. In so doing, they build organisational capacity that produces significant company results. Sinek outlines a philosophy that has gained a lot of traction over recent years, which says you should lead the people, not the numbers, and that leaders take responsibility for lives, not profit and loss reports.

Management guru Peter Drucker, in his 1946 book *Concept of the Corporation*, described a theory he called Decentralisation of Management. His view was that many business leaders would attempt to assume all responsibilities as a display of power or to maintain a level of control, suggesting that they were the only ones capable of undertaking those responsibilities. Central to

Drucker's huge body of work was the concept that to create a successful corporation, entrepreneurs and managers must delegate tasks to empower employees.

Drucker features heavily in MBA programs around the world, and Sinek is one of the most watched business experts on the internet. Their message is clear. If you are going to be successful in building a tribe, you must decentralise power and focus on the development of others. To do this effectively, start with your behaviours, your communication and your development and, like a ripple in a pond, watch the impact roll out from there.

Inspire confidence

The people stuff is the topic of discussion that most often comes up in my mentor meetings with entrepreneurial business owners.

Staff are human and can be emotional and unpredictable; structure helps to manage them.

When we are discussing how we build capability and invest in our people through training, I often get the question, 'What happens if we spend all this money and they leave?' I always give the same response, 'What if we don't spend this money and they stay?'

Not everyone in an organisation aspires to climb the ladder and go through middle management and on to senior management. And the good news is that we don't want them to. Having people with different levels of ambition is critical to have a balanced workforce that isn't made up entirely of chiefs, and often expensive ones. We need people who are conscientious, people who are intuitive, and people who are ready and willing to complement those who are more ambitious.

It takes a range of different and diverse individuals to make a team hum. The key is to play to strengths and be inclusive. Take the time to connect with your people as individuals and align their aspirations with those of the organisation. I have found that one of the most effective tools to build capability and maximise the potential of every person is to formalise individual growth and career plans. These are personalised documents that map out a personal and professional journey that plays to strengths, facilitates purpose and aligns with values. A specific development plan should provide the right cocktail of inspiration, training, support, mentoring and feedback.

Great teams celebrate the contribution of individuals whose behaviour aligns with team standards. For this to happen, you must first set the bar and communicate the acceptable standards to the tribe. Each person must be keenly aware of their specific role, how it fits in the broader team and how it contributes to the organisational outcomes. They must be aware of where their delegated authority – those boundaries that define their autonomy and decision making in the role – starts and finishes. They must understand where they fit within their team and, above all, they must feel safe.

In his book *The Culture Code*, Daniel Coyle says that a critical element of feeling safe is to positively interpret belonging cues. In doing so we ask three basic questions.

> *'Do we share a future? Are we connected? Are we safe?'*

Coyle cites the findings from a Stanford University study in which middle school students were asked to write an essay, for which teachers provided different types of feedback. Researchers identified the numerous types of feedback, one of which they called 'magical feedback'. The feedback included the statement, 'I'm giving you these comments because I have very high expectations and I know that you can reach them.' Students who received this type of feedback chose to revise their paper far more than students who did not, and their performance improved significantly.

According to Coyle, this feedback was successful and effective because it provides three specific belonging cues. They are:

1. You are part of the group.
2. This group is special; we have high standards here.
3. I believe you can reach those standards.

Coyle argues that these cues play directly to our unconscious brain, telling us this is a safe place to give effort.

Feedback provided in this way can be written, verbal or expressed through body language. The first cue is personal and translates as 'You are supported and I care about you.' The second is performance feedback that indicates where the bar is set in the organisation, and that we have high standards. The third plays to a bigger picture and translates that together we are playing a bigger game than this specific example. These cues create confidence, and when we are confident, we perform better.

When I read this in Coyle's book, it really resonated with me. I remember that as a young boy of six or seven all I wanted to do was play cricket for Australia. I would spend all summer listening to the test match on a transistor radio, and hitting a golf ball off a wall with a cricket stump for hours on end.

One summer holiday my parents sent me off to a three-day

cricket camp run by former Australian cricketers. The memories of those three days are vivid even now. I can still feel the burning sun on my arms, the ache in my back as I woke up, raring to go, on day three of the camp after bowling and batting my heart out. I also remember the awe I felt throughout the camp in getting to meet some of my sporting heroes. It was one of the highlights of my childhood.

There was one incident from that camp that is etched in my memory and still makes me smile today. We were doing a catching drill, and many of the kids were scared of getting hurt by the hard cricket ball. Ian Callan, a former Australian and Victorian cricketer, was conducting the drill and hitting the ball high in the air. Each kid would take it in turns to come forward from the line some fifty metres away, park themselves under the sky-high, arcing cricket ball, and attempt to catch it. Most kids dropped it. Some made it look like they were attempting to catch the ball, but went nowhere near it so they wouldn't hurt their hands.

I too was worried about the pain of the ball hitting my hands and concerned that, should I drop it, I would look silly in front of the other kids and one of my sporting heroes. Then it was my turn. The ball made a loud crack as it hit the bat and went what seemed like miles in the air. I nervously parked myself under it, waiting for gravity to take hold and send the ball rapidly downwards towards my tiny hands. I held my cupped hands up, faced the sky above, and waited. As the ball smashed into my palms, there was a little give in my hands that cushioned the blow. I had caught the ball!

I still remember the feeling of the hard leather ball as it sat nestled in my hands. I confidently threw it back as my hero loudly proclaimed to the group, 'Great catch, Chris has hands as safe as houses.' I didn't miss another catch that day. The bar had been set, the belonging cues simply and clearly articulated, and belief was instilled. Interestingly, I went on to be a very good catch and have played cricket right up to this very day. I credit that one comment, which has stuck with me all my life, for giving me that belief.

If we are confident, we can do amazing things!

When I examine the power of this day in light of Coyle's work, it makes sense. Like the students who received the empowering feedback as part of the Stanford experiment, I was made to feel part of a group of good catchers. This group had high standards, and because the feedback came from someone I greatly admired and respected, the belief stuck. I was inspired, I had built belief, and in doing so I had built capacity in a fundamentally critical part of the game.

If you as an entrepreneur can harness the power of these principles of feedback in supporting the growth of your people, you will be a long way towards building organisational capability that will see you achieve your vision of a scalable business.

When your people understand where the bar is set and know that you believe they can meet those standards, this will drive engagement and discretionary effort. In achieving this it is critical that you have a no-blame culture and everyone feels safe in taking accountability for their role. Just like the students in the Stanford University experiment or my experience at a summer cricket camp, belief and safety, when combined with constructive feedback and support, provides a potent cocktail that can rapidly and effectively build the capability of your team and your business. When your team is confident and you are confident in your team, creating a business by design becomes a whole lot easier.

Challenge groupthink

One of the greatest business mentors you may never have heard of is Bill Campbell. An ex-American college football coach, Bill forged an influential career in mentoring and coaching some of America's biggest and most successful companies. Companies such as Apple, Google and Intuit.

In his book *Trillion Dollar Coach*, Eric Schmidt (et al) provides example after example of when Campbell was able to guide a conversation through a business-need lens and soar above individual agendas. In doing this, he was able to drive superior business outcomes to extraordinary effect. Part of Bill Campbell's success was his ability to help decision makers view issues through multiple lenses, and so free them from emotion, self-protection and positive-enhancement bias. Of course, the leaders of these organisations have gone on to be revered and some, like Steve Jobs, have become legendary household names.

Given our natural inclination to revere famous individuals, it is fascinating to note that none of the leaders of these legendary companies did it alone. They had a band of strong strategic thinkers, including Bill Campbell, who were able to metaphorically get their people to stand on the desk and see decision making and situations from multiple angles. This multi-dimensional, contextual framing of a problem helps to overcome a contradictory instinct we have as humans. We are biased towards self-protection and self-enhancement, and winning the approval of the group supports these biases. Therefore, our natural inclination is to elevate the view of others in the room above our own. I'll say that again, our evolutionary bias is to defer to others and elevate their view in the room over our own.

> *This natural inclination towards groupthink is dangerous in a business environment.*

The ability to challenge our desire to fit in is critical to drive effective organisational strategy and good decision making. An absence of multiple views and opinions means that you and your leaders are making key decisions based on emotion, gut feel and limited contextual information tainted by evolutionary bias.

It is critical that leaders create awareness of these biases and seek differing contextual views if we are to make more decisions that lead to business success. Naturally, you as owner tend to be the biggest and most influential voice in the room.

It is also critical, to make effective and balanced decisions, that you are aware of evolutionary bias and call out your people to truly get a diversity of views and maximise the available information. It is healthy to surround ourselves with people who are prepared to challenge our thinking and come at issues from different angles and perspectives. In collecting a range of diverse views and looking at issues through multiple lenses, we will have the tools to stare down our evolutionary wiring and make richer, more constructive decisions.

In his book *Outliers*, Malcolm Gladwell wrote of the potential impact of evolutionary bias and cultural hierarchies through his Korean Air case study. In the 80s and 90s, Korean Air had more crashes than any other airline in the world. Despite modern planes, highly trained pilots and perfect flying conditions, there was still a significant number of crashes. Why? It turns out that the co-pilots were often aware of errors being made by the pilot that would ultimately lead to crashes, but the power differential and hierarchy was so ingrained they were fearful of speaking up. The planes were designed to be flown by equals, but in Korean culture you are obliged to be deferential to your elders. As such, co-pilots never questioned their captains – to catastrophic effect. As entrepreneurial business owners, we too must be mindful that we do not lead the herd in groupthink. It is by encouraging participation, fostering a culture of inclusion and providing people with opportunities to speak up and contribute that we will develop our teams more effectively and make better business decisions on our way through the entrepreneurial ceiling.

You might be wondering what happened to the structural steel company, which we highlighted at the start of this chapter, after 2008. Fast-forward to 2022. The company is quite the success story and the investment in its people has paid handsome dividends. This business has increased its revenue by eleven-fold since that difficult period. It has continued to evolve and moved further upstream by merging with trusted partners to vertically integrate and own its supply chain.

The company is now a one-stop shop for government infrastructure projects that are looking for a trusted partner with the demonstrated capabilities to design, engineer, model, build, erect and clad. It has completed some of Australia's largest infrastructure projects. And yes, it continues to invest in the future and has a well-defined strategic direction. This business has tactical clarity around how it competes and continues to invest and build capacity in its people. It has gone on to become one of Australia's great business success stories.

What will you do today to ensure you have the right people tomorrow to drive your business by design?

BREAKTHROUGH
BITES

- As a breakthrough business owner looking to build a business by design, it is essential that you rethink the organisational structure of your business and align individual capabilities with your strategic direction.

- For thousands of years, mankind has congregated in groups and collectively worked together to better the tribe, with each individual playing to their strengths to harness the collective skill for the good of the community.

- It's not enough that our quest provides us with purpose, it must inspire our people as well.

- It is critical that each individual understands their role and value in achieving the collective good.

- The most fundamental of entrepreneurial issues that keeps a business below the ceiling and stops breakthrough is, invariably, you the entrepreneur.

- The key ingredient that supports the shift in you is confidence; however, the paradox you face is that you can't become confident without letting go!

- To move through the entrepreneurial ceiling and get out of the weeds, you will need to effectively leverage the knowledge you have garnered and developed.

- Staff are human and can be emotional and unpredictable; structure helps to manage them.

- The natural inclination towards groupthink is dangerous in a business environment.

7

Tread your Own Path

Is good enough

J im Collins' book *Good to Great* studied S&P 500 companies and identified five characteristics of commercially success-ful and sustainable businesses and the stages of the journey that they took. He used the metaphor of trying to turn a big concrete flywheel. It takes a lot of work and effort to get it moving, but once it gains momentum it's very difficult to stop.

Good to Great is a wonderful book and has fantastic lessons for you as a business owner, but is it relevant if you don't want to grow your business to the size of a publicly listed company, or even become a high growth company? I would argue that the structures and journey outlined in Collins' book have relevance no matter the size or aspirations of the business, but not all businesses will need or want to go from good to great. Good is sometimes enough.

Many of the examples I have used in this book have been businesses I have mentored that looked to grow significantly, and go from a small to medium size business to a larger, family-corporate style. While this is the ambition for many, it's not the ambition for all. As Scott Pape, the Barefoot Investor is fond of saying, 'Tread your own path.'

I mentor a dairy distribution business in a large regional centre in Victoria. I was thrilled to be asked to work with this business. I have vivid memories of the milkman delivering fresh milk in tin foil-topped glass bottles to our doorstep in suburban Melbourne when I was a child in the early 70s. It was my job to put out the empty bottles in a wire basket the night before. I would often wake in the morning to the clip clop of the milkman's massive Clydesdale horses taking him on his rounds. I would rush out of bed to ensure I could open the first bottle and taste the cream sitting waiting for me on top of the milk.

The modern dairy distribution business is a very different business from the one I have fond memories of as a child. It is more a warehousing, freight and logistics business. A time- and temperature-critical business that requires efficient organisation and timed-to-the-minute processes to bring it all together.

My client does not have significant growth aspirations, but the journey through the entrepreneurial ceiling is just as relevant to her as it is to businesses that have their sights firmly set on building to a family-corporate model of high growth.

This dairy distributor distributes milk, cheese, cream and other perishable products to cafés, food service centres, restaurants, businesses and schools. The business was founded in 1985 and has been owned and operated by the founder's daughter since 2015. It is a wonderful family business, much loved in the region where it operates. The owner is known for her warmth, friendly smile, dedication to her customers and heart of gold.

The business was associated with a local dairy cooperative that held market dominance since it began. The local brand was so strong there was little need to undertake marketing or cus-tomer generation activities. Most consumers simply preferred their products. That all changed in 2017, when the local milk production company made the decision to close the factory and stop producing the local brand. The distributor that had been instrumental in growing and championing the brand was effectively out of business through circumstances beyond her control.

The owner and her team of three administrative staff and eleven drivers were devastated. They had six months to find a new supplier, but it wouldn't be easy. Many of the national brands were already distributed by other companies in the region. The distributor would not only have to find a new brand and products to distribute, she would have to convince her existing client base to adopt those products. What had been a relatively secure and stable business was about to get much tougher.

Over the next six months the owner interviewed suppliers and identified a brand from southern New South Wales she believed represented her concept of 'local', which the business had prided itself on as a key point of difference for thirty-two years. Once changeover occurred, competition for milk and dairy distribution became manic. A mad dash by distributors of national brands to win customers saw discounting and switching incentives flood the market like never before.

This had significant impact on the distributor. Cashflow fell dramatically and began to dry up, sales and marketing, which had hardly warranted a mention before, became incredibly important. Demand waned as the distributor desperately scrambled to establish a new brand and retain clients in her traditional market.

She was now firmly entrenched under the entrepreneurial ceiling. She did not have the business systems, the people capability or the knowledge to compete in a hyper-competitive market. She had never had to. Without adequate business systems and efficiencies, the business was chaotic in the day to day. The distributor was overwhelmed by customer demands, aggressive competitors and the financial burden of having a business that was over-geared for what was required to deliver the now smaller supply volumes. The dairy industry, in particular the milk distribution sector, operates on paper-thin margins, with the whole model designed to shift volume. That volume had now gone.

The business had two premises, eleven trucks and a lot of slow-moving inventory. With milk volumes decreasing and many price-sensitive customers migrating to other suppliers, sales of food service products also declined dramatically. The owner knew she had to do something, but where to start? Life under the entrepreneurial ceiling was not sustainable, and she was running out of cash fast. The business relied too heavily on her in the day-to-day operations, and she knew it.

In 2018, the owner adopted a breakthrough attitude and set about rebuilding the business from the ground up.

She consolidated the operation into one premise. She sold off old trucks that were surplus to needs and redesigned her truck runs to be more efficient. Three drivers retired or left and were not replaced. She visited other distribution centres in capital cities to learn how they operated. She built a winning team and hired a dedicated operations manager who could bring efficiency to the logistics, maintain the vehicles and manage the drivers. She went to work with her new supplier and together they put a sales representative on the ground and held client relationship events to show their appreciation for 'supporting local'. She drafted operations manuals and implemented vehicle management technology. Most recently, she hired a marketing and administration employee to bolster her marketing firepower.

She was now a different leader, a different person. She committed to change and made it happen.

As these initiatives started to take shape and the financial position of the business improved, the owner upgraded her fleet with more efficient and capable trucks, which were better set up to service the volumes the business was now doing. She set up a rainy-day account to squirrel away funds to undertake continuous business improvement and drive efficiencies.

Although she had no significant growth aspirations for the business, she did have a clear vision. A local business that excelled at customer service. A local business that existed to service locals. She was determined to provide a great place to work for her team and herself. She didn't need the business to be great. Good was enough.

Everything was going well, and the owner had done a remarkable job in turning her business around in two short years. Then, in March 2020, COVID hit. Hospitality businesses, which represented the bulk of her customers, were forced to close. This was the ultimate audit on the efficiencies she had implemented over the previous two years. Although tough, the business was able to survive the next two years until everything reopened. The systems, processes and people she had put in place held up. Good was indeed good enough.

Not all business owners aspire to create mega family-corporate companies, but rather, they aspire to create a business by design that provides a good income for them and their employees.

Such a business that is not operationally reliant is an enjoyable place to work, functions with the level of input the owners want and aligns with their purpose and values.

To break through the entrepreneurial ceiling and build your business by design, you will need a number of fundamentals in your armoury. Like the concrete slab of a house on which all else is built upon, these fundamentals will provide the foundations for your journey and the bedrock on which your business by design can be built – no matter how grand or humble your aspiration may be.

Define what's important

We hear a lot about defining values in business literature. But it can be hard to understand how, by doing that, you will gain greater benefit than by focusing on the operational, chaotic business of the day to day.

> *Part of the challenge in trying to align your life and business with what is truly important to you is figuring out what your values are and then prioritising actions accordingly.*

For many of you, taking the time to stop and reflect rather than motor on at a hundred miles per hour is uncomfortable. It is uncomfortable because it requires significant self-reflection to deep dive into what is truly important. Anyway, who has time to waste doing this when there are so many more important tasks to do in the day to day? You have a to-do list you can't jump over and a million emails that require a response, and you're already swamped without taking on another thing.

The good news is that it is when you are stressed, mentally in the worst place you could be and confronting the direst of circumstances, that you learn the most and understand what you truly value. I know it doesn't sound like good news, but as Michael Voss, the AFL three-time premiership legend, Brownlow Medalist and Carlton coach said, 'You learn nothing from holding up premiership cups, you learn the most in your darkest day.'

Dr Kelly McGonigal, PhD, in her book *The Upside of Stress*, has taken a different approach to the black and white notion that stress is bad and being stress-free is good. She explores various studies that have found that stress is bad, and argues that it is not necessarily the stress itself that does the damage, but rather the meaning we attach to it. In fact, she believes that stress is critical to experience a full, challenging, goal-orientated life. The most commonly reported sources of stress overlap with the greatest sources of meaning we have in life. If this is the case, then stress may even contribute to our wellbeing. Looking for meaning in what we define as stressful may provide insights and breakthroughs.

So how do we go about defining our values? I like the Traction model by Gino Wickman. Wickman suggests that to define our values in a business context, we should think of three people who, if we cloned them, would lead to market domination. Pick people you personally admire and whom you respect. What are their characteristics? What do you most admire about them? What is it about them that would lead to market domination? List the words that come to mind.

Once you have your list of characteristics, do a bit of wordsmithing and combine words with similar meaning to reduce your list. Now score each word out of ten, with ten being those words that most resonate with what you believe, and one being words that don't align with what is important in your personal view as well as your business perspective. Sometimes it's valuable to do this exercise with your team to get buy-in and encourage behaviours that align with the values.

Next, take your top four or five scoring words and draft a sentence that explains what that word means to your organisation and why it is important.

Now that you have done the heavy lifting and identified your organisational values, it is time to live them in the day to day. Celebrating behaviours that align with the organisational values and managing behaviours that do not allows you, as the owner, to set the standards. Standards that will ultimately set the bar around who you are and what you do as an organisation. Standards that you can build upon that will facilitate accountability as the business transitions through the entrepreneurial ceiling to a more disciplined and accountable business by design.

Having set the organisational values and used these to define expectations and behaviours, you now have the tools to have the right conversations with yourself and your team. Conversations that create alignment between what we will do and where we are going. As Susan Scott described them in her book *Fierce Conversations*, these are conversations enabled through common language, a bigger-picture focus and shared understanding of what is acceptable. They are free from emotion and focused on process. They are game-changing.

Get financially literate

Financial reporting, modelling and budgeting are activities that many entrepreneurs struggle with. Many of you see these processes as a waste of time, given that the guesstimates and assumptions that form the basis of this work are often inaccurate and, therefore, irrelevant. Reporting represents what has happened in the past. It's a rear-mirror view that does little to help with current events. What's done is done.

The reality is that numbers are the language of business, and even if you aspire to a good business rather than a Jim Collins-style great business, it will be challenging to transition through the entrepreneurial ceiling without having a fundamental understanding of what your numbers are telling you.

You may also struggle to read financial statements and reporting. You see the numbers, but interpreting them in the business context and then trying to use them in decision making can be challenging.

The value of budgeting in an SME business can also be unclear for many entrepreneurs. Budgeting as a process has two distinct angles. First, it forces the business to consider where its revenue will come from. Questions include what pricing model it should adopt, what an attractive customer avatar does and doesn't look like, and what distribution channels it could explore.

The second element of the budget relates to business expenditure. In considering expenditure, you must choose very carefully where you will allocate scarce resources. Considering direct costs, variable costs, overheads and capital expenditure in light of anticipated revenue enables you to explore what-if scenarios. In doing so, you can better understand the potential impacts of decision making.

> *Financial modelling is about strategic choice. About choosing one strategic direction over another. Often it is not what actions you go forward with, but rather which strategic options you leave on the cutting room floor.*

By undertaking a robust budgeting process, you will better understand the opportunity cost of deliberately allocating resources to one area of the business at the expense of another. It is a discipline that forces you to decide how you will or will not compete, choose what competitive advantages you will invest in and consider how the market may react. No matter the type of business or the industry in which you compete, budgeting forces the entrepreneurial business to focus intent and consider alternative views when utilising scarce resources.

Budgets are a fantastic business tool and can be applied for both planning and organisational control. When combined with monthly or quarterly reporting, you can assess and learn from the results and adjust strategically and operationally to meet the market conditions. As a control tool, the budgeting process provides checks and balances that reduce leakage. This drops more of the profits to the bottom line. Further, effective budgeting enables you to confidently invest in capital to increase capability, drive strategic intent and foster competitive advantage. Having a budget is like having a football game scoreboard, and can drive real focus!

Modern accounting software packages make it easy for you to review and manage budgets. When you're getting started, or if you're not sure how to do something, you can save time by using the skills of your accountant. They are wonderful resources to support your financial literacy and help put in place the reporting and processes that inform your decision making.

No matter what size your business is, or whether you wish to go from good to great or are happy to be good enough, getting through the entrepreneurial ceiling will be easier if you have the practical ability to speak the language of business... numbers.

Get out of your head

You need to get out of your head in two ways. The first is to record the knowledge in your head so that others can do that task and become bolder. The second is to stop overthinking things to the point of procrastination or, worse, paralysis. Get moving.

Let's start with getting knowledge out of your head. Traditionally, that would have been an operation manual, training program, white paper, or anything that takes what you know and puts it in a form others can follow. In the modern era, there is an endless stream of software applications that make this possible.

The first thing you need is time. To get you going, allocate 'big rocks time' and be bloody-minded in protecting it. Set up this time like you would a project. Start with the simplest tasks you do and probably shouldn't be doing. I don't want my CEO sweeping the floor, and I am sure you can find plenty of examples of this sort of work that you can document quickly and get off your plate.

If you're having trouble getting started, there is even an app for that. Try playing background music or use a background noise app like Coffivity. Set a timer for twenty minutes and get into flow.

Over time you will create a templated process, be it via software or some other means, for capturing the information you know and disseminating it to the team. Many people find it useful to simply video or screen-record information and store it in a searchable, indexed library that can be accessed via a smartphone or tablet. If you can make a task less arduous and even fun, you are more likely to do it.

If, after capturing the information in your process, you find there is still a significant gap between what you know and the capability of the company to execute it without you, this may indicate a skill gap you need to either recruit or train for.

Once you have your information-recording system humming, it's time to get your team involved and have them capture the information that is in *their* heads. Over time, this process of sys-temising a business creates performance consistency, which is a key element of life on the other side of the entrepreneurial ceiling. Not only that, if you're looking to sell, scale or replicate your business in the future, you will have created real value in your business model.

The second way you need to get out of your head is to not over-think things. I am not saying take risks without considering the consequences, but in my experience the businesses that grow, regardless of what that looks like for them, have owners who are prepared to back themselves and their team. Business owners who are a little bold, daring and courageous, who understand that calculated risk is part of growing a business, are more likely to succeed than those that sit on their hands.

But at what point does risk tolerance become reckless?

It's a great question, but unfortunately there is no one-size-fits-all answer. What I suggest is to expose yourself to as many business leaders of the modern era, and over history, as you can. Don't just focus on those who have won big; sometimes we learn more from those who have failed than we do from those who have succeeded. Ted Talks, business books, autobiographies, documentaries and podcasts are all great ways to expand your thinking and set your own risk tolerance levels.

The other thing I suggest is to find a mentor or two with whom you can bounce ideas around. Every great businessperson or successful entrepreneur has a person or two helping in the background. I have always found it inspiring, and a great investment, to have a coach or mentor whom I can turn to shift perspective or reframe and test ideas. My clients, I am sure, would say the same.

Create new habits and rituals

It should be no surprise that if you want a different result, you need to do things differently. If you are to get out of the weeds and get on with building a business by design, it must happen in the minutia of the moment in the day to day.

James Clear is the author of *Atomic Habits*, which has sold over five million copies and been translated into more than fifty languages. He identified that your life today is essentially the sum of your habits. It naturally follows that where you are today, in life and in business, is the result of what you have done in the past. It also follows that what you do today will dictate the results you get tomorrow. Given this, creating positive, impactful habits that serve you and align with what you wish to achieve are critical if you are to build a different business model and create a business and life by design.

As we have discussed, the challenge with long-term goals – like building a business by design and breaking through the entrepreneurial ceiling – is that it takes time, and we are wired for short-term rewards. If you can align your lifestyle and working environments with productive habits, you can build a sustainable operating rhythm that creates momentum and positive activity. As with anything worthwhile, however, you are not likely to see significant results in the short term. And this is challenging for us humans.

Going to the gym and doing 3 x 30 reps of weights will not result in anything other than sore arms for a few of days or even a few weeks. However, doing this four times a week over a year will bring extraordinary change.

> *A habit executed over a long period will bring long-term results.*

Referring to business achievement, Tony Robbins famously said, 'We naturally overestimate what can be achieved in a year and underestimate what we could achieve in ten years.' Having had the privilege to mentor so many businesses' journeys through the entrepreneurial ceiling, I have watched this play out time and time again.

Business owners who have created the habits, rituals and routines that change their reality have been able to extricate themselves from the business tasks and processes that kept them firmly stuck under the entrepreneurial ceiling. They have gone on to create good businesses that provided them with the business and life by design they desired.

Let's revisit our regional dairy distribution business. The business has recovered after COVID in line with the hospitality industry, but the biggest shift I have witnessed is in the owner. She has a determination to transition through the entrepreneurial ceiling by creating a system-driven working environment that moves information out of her head, and her key people's heads, into a defined operating system.

She has partnered with a wonderful accountant who has taken the time to help her understand the financial position of the business and educate her on financial literacy and business performance indicators.

She has invested heavily in cloud-based, affordable IT platforms, plus the external support to maximise their impact. These systems are not only changing the way the business operates and driving efficiencies, they are also shifting the means by which customers order. Like the bank ATM machines of the 80s, they enable a self-service model customers enjoy using while removing labour costs from the ordering process.

Additional, unexpected benefits have also become apparent. These include increased average customer spend, accelerated uptake of new product lines and efficiencies created by gamifying the ordering process.

While the odd manual order pad can still be seen in the business, the focus on creating a business by design has provided new freedoms for this entrepreneurial business owner, revolutionised the efficiency of the operation and reduced its reliance on the owner.

The biggest win for this multi-generational, family-based business, which was built on customer service and client connection, is that the owner was able to create a brave new world without compromising what is important. She has created new operating systems while being mindful of maintaining the values that she and this business hold dear. She has retained the cultural idiosyncrasies that define her business, and in doing so has honoured the legacy left by her family.

Growing big businesses is not the right path for every entrepreneur. Sometimes, good is enough.

BREAKTHROUGH
BITES

- Not all business owners aspire to create mega family-corporate companies, but rather look to create a business by design that provides a good income for them and their employees.

- Part of the challenge in trying to align your life and business with what is truly important to you is figuring out what your values are and then prioritising actions accordingly.

- The value of budgeting in an SME can be unclear for many entrepreneurs.

- A budget helps you consider where your revenue is coming from and how much of this you will keep.

- Financial modelling is about strategic choice and choosing one direction over another. Often it is not what actions you go forward with, but rather which strategic options you leave on the cutting room floor.

- Business owners who are a little bold, daring and courageous, and who understand calculated risk as part of growing a business, are more likely to succeed.

- A habit executed over a long period will bring long-term results.

- It should be no surprise that if you want a different result, you need to do things differently.

- Growing big businesses is not the right path for every entrepreneur. Sometimes good is enough.

8

Get Out of
Your Way

Change lanes

reg McKeown, in his book *Essentialism,* says, 'Life by design is not life by default.' The same goes for business by design. It can't be a business by default; however, the reality is that most are. To create a business by design you must undertake deliberate actions and processes that align with your priorities. Working harder and hoping that things will change by tinkering around the edges will not get it done. You must decide what you want, shift the behaviour of yourself and your team, build process and business systems away from yourself and be single minded in getting it done.

It must be a total shift of action and attitude that means you only focus on those things that align with your aspirations. This is easier said than done but there are things you can do that will make it simpler to achieve. Once we have truly made the decision to do things differently, we must align our working environment accordingly. Rather than rely on willpower to stay the course, you can hack your working environment in such a way that the shift happens in spite of you.

In her book *The Willpower Instinct,* Stanford Professor Dr Kelly McGonigal says, 'When your mind is preoccupied, your impulses – not your long-term goals – will guide your choices.' This is a problem for entrepreneurs, because preoccupation can be a default mode when so many things are coming at you at once.

> *The great news is that there are things you can do to get through the entrepreneurial ceiling without having to rely on willpower alone.*

In 2014, I started mentoring a small regional business that specialised in modelling and drafting, predominantly in structural steel applications. The business was part of another business that started in 2005 and included mechanical engineering. It was obvious the two businesses would be better off separated, and in 2015 they parted ways and a new entity was born. At this time, the business consisted of four employees plus the executive leader.

While there were some clients who moved to the newly created business, many were looking for mechanical engineering services and stayed with the business that retained the original name. The split was extremely amicable, and initially the two businesses operated from the same premises. Not long afterwards, however, the business I was mentoring decided to make the split completely and set up purpose-built facilities closer to the centre of town.

These first few years were a struggle as the fledgling break-away business looked to build the systems and processes it required. The business relied heavily on the owner and was in a high growth phase. The growth was exciting, and the business was highly reactive to the demands of the client base. The work was always time-sensitive, but the owner and a loyal following of employees got the job done, albeit by working long hours.

Success continued and the business moved past the rewarding growth phase and into to the chaotic phase under the entrepreneurial ceiling, where they were still highly reactive to customer demands, but now it wasn't so much fun. By 2017, there was more work than the business could do, and it lacked enough staff due to its location in a regional centre. While the owner was by nature a calm individual, it was clear the unrelenting workload and customer demands were getting to him. He felt totally overwhelmed and could not see a way that he could satisfy his customers without burning out himself and his people.

Attracting skilled recruits was challenging, as most with this skillset lived in capital cities. A client base that had previously loved what the business offered was now frustrated with the delays and inaccuracies that were costing them time and money. The owner could see his exposure to having to pay significant damages for rework was growing and he was worried. The long hours were taking its toll and his home life was suffering. He was in a bad place and felt like he was under siege from all angles.

It was at this time that the owner met with me at Melbourne Airport as we transitioned between appointments. He outlined the chaos and overwhelm of his world. Over the next two hours, among the busyness of people coming and going in an airport café, we worked up a mind map of a future direction for the business. We created the foundations for transition that would, over time, take the business from chaos to scalable. By the end of our session, a very relieved business owner left Melbourne Airport with a plan. A plan for breakthrough.

While the company had some really dedicated employees on the ground, a lot of information was in the owner's head. We started a process of capturing key information in an operating manual, groomed a future star of the business by getting him to oversee the project, and also created a structured human resources system.

While this began the breakthrough process, the key issue remained labour. In 2018, we undertook a planning process using Wickman's Entrepreneurial Operating System (Traction) and mapped a path for future expansion. Although the owner seemed to enthusiastically embrace the concept of geographic expansion to access the skilled labour the business so desperately required, in reality he wasn't really convinced. He was nervous about the investment required to execute the plan. As a result, when he returned to the day to day, his commitment rapidly waned and the plan ended up gathering metaphoric dust on the shelf.

The day-to-day chaos and overwhelm continued with business as usual. Finally, having run out of options, we reconvened with key people in the organisation and, in August of 2018, we committed to look overseas for staff. To better understand what was involved, we went on a road trip and met with another client of mine from Melbourne that had undertaken this process. By the start of 2019, the business had a Philippines division.

The overseas division was meant to bolster productivity and output, but it didn't. What it *did* do was highlight system deficiencies and rework issues. Over the next three years, the company would expand the overseas team, contract it, put on a senior person at double the cost to oversee them on the ground, and allocate a full-time resource to manage and support the team from the Australian end. But no matter what we did, performance was inconsistent and quality issues were a constant. Far from helping the chaos and overwhelm, the Philippines division exacerbated it. Further, the business was drifting. It was not committed to a clear aspiration or objective, but rather everyone was fighting fires in the day to day. Although still growing, the team was over capacity, overwhelmed and over it. Time to reconvene!

For many businesses, the continuous struggles of an underperforming remote division would have been seen as a disaster – a bottomless money pit that had not yielded the results the business hoped for. But that was not the case for this business. The challenges the overseas division created had, in fact, galvanised both the decision to change and the impetus to make the shift.

It was the catalyst to take a system focus and build layers of leadership under the entrepreneur. Specialist software and operating processes, manuals and procedures were developed. The second in charge, who became a partner in 2018, stepped up and there was no longer a key-person risk in the form of the entrepreneurial leader. The business had broken through transition to the leveraged, developmental phase, then went on to become a consistent, systems-driven and sustainable business.

While the overseas division and the inability to gain efficiencies had been a catalyst for change, the big shift had in fact been the decision to commit to a future direction and drive the initiatives at every level of the business. Again, following the Traction model, in 2019 and into 2020 a new vision was established and driven by structured meetings, called 'Level 10' meetings, that took place throughout the business. These meetings were a ritual for this business and a key driver of change. Issues were identified, discussed and solved as a team. Actions and key priorities were committed to and accountabilities focused on each week. The business made the decision to be different and implemented the processes to make it happen.

If it was not in their future plan, it did not exist. The entrepreneurial owner had decided to change, had set up an environment and operating systems that took him out of the loop and, as a result, the business made the shift. He and his offsider had moved the culture from working harder to working on what mattered. They changed the internal belief that working harder was a badge of honour, and rewarded those who focused effort using the Level 10 process – where big rocks were scheduled, weekly actions were made visible and people were held accountable for what they committed to.

This internal process, which creates decision making based on what matters and not what is urgent, led to the closing of the overseas division in late 2020. A new, focused push then began looking to the longer-term goal of growing their own talent through a training and cadet program, which has to this day achieved outstanding results.

This story highlights that, until you truly decide to follow a different path and commit that decision, the journey through the entrepreneurial ceiling cannot commence. This business started the journey through the ceiling almost accidently, driven by a regional labour shortage. But they committed to action and decided to do things differently. The thing that stands out to me is that they did not photocopy the same day and stick their heads in the sand, hoping something different would happen. They committed to working on the business and looked for a less conventional path rather than accept the status quo. They looked outside the box, and in doing so transitioned through the entrepreneurial ceiling to create a system-driven and sustainable business with minimal key-person risk. All key elements required for creating a business by design.

Now let's look at some clever ideas I have seen others implement to eliminate the need to base transition through the entrepreneurial ceiling on willpower. We know from Dr McGonigal's work that any long-term goal built on willpower alone is likely to fail. The following actions provide insight and ideas on how you can create an organisational environment that effectively progresses towards your business by design – in spite of you.

Like the example above, creating an environment that implements fundamentals of a breakthrough business that do not rely on you, has more chance of success. After all, what got you to today will not get you to tomorrow. The major issue with truly making the shift to breakthrough is the constant in the journey: you.

While the previous chapters have been about how you personally, and quite rightly, influence breakthrough, this chapter is about setting up the environment to create the ideal circumstances to enable organisational momentum. Like a petri dish in a laboratory, you need the right conditions to facilitate and change behaviours in both yourself and your team. These must focus on what matters if they are to ultimately drive breakthrough.

Make it a precedent

Legal cases can be complex. No two cases, whether criminal or civil, are ever the same. The complex business of ensuring the punishment fits the crime would be almost impossible to do consistently without relying on legal precedent. That is, the outcomes and rulings of previous cases are adopted as the guide for similar future cases. It is the job of the lawyers to argue that one precedent is more relevant than another, and achieve the most effective outcome for their clients by aligning the circumstances of a case to precedent cases.

Just like a legal precedent, the ability to apply a decision precedent when choices and decisions have to be made in the day-to-day business is incredibly useful in staying the course and creating a business by design.

If you have to make a decision every single time you are confronted with a similar situation, you will most likely choose the path of least resistance rather than the path that will provide the best outcome in the longer term.

It can be like crossing a busy intersection. We all know that when the little man flashes red we shouldn't start to cross the road, and if we're in no particular hurry most of us simply wait for the little man to turn green. If we absolutely need to be somewhere and are on the clock, many of us step out against the flashing red man.

Like stepping off the curb when the red man is flashing, many of you will take the path of least resistance and do work that should be delegated to someone else if you're busy and under pressure. The problem with this is that it does not serve our long-term aspirations of building capability in others and reducing key-person risk. We perpetuate the single point of failure. At the very least you are likely to be inconsistent in how you go about creating capacity in others and applying the systems that enable this. You will tinker around the edges of what you know you must do until, very quickly, the opportunity to shift is gone and any potential change has lost impact.

The trick is to have a set of rules, or precedents, prepared that take away the need to make a decision in the moment. Precedents guide what type of work you will delegate; they're about sticking to the business systems and following rules. Set rules so that when temptation hits, you don't have to make a decision – the precedent you have predetermined will dictate the action.

You can use precedent-setting in all sorts of scenarios. Delegating work (right person, right job), qualifying customers, taking breaks, creating boundaries around what you will and will not do. Productivity expert Dermott Crowley has created masterful precedents around how to maximise productivity in a world where emails come at you all the time. I have adopted Crowley's model and tailored it to my situation.

I start by only dealing with email at predetermined times. If the email can be responded to quickly, I deal with it and file it out of my inbox. If it will take more than five minutes, I schedule it in my diary. If it is irrelevant, I delete it. This simple process, or precedent, for how I handle email eliminates decision making that can lead down a bottomless rabbit hole. After all, the more you send the more you get back. It's the ultimate perpetual motion machine if not dealt with in a structured way.

You spend a lot of time in business making decisions. This can lead to decision fatigue that saps your energy. As we have discussed, the porpoising effect under the entrepreneurial ceiling is predicated upon energy. The more we spend, the less we have. The less we have, the more likely we are to be in a state of overwhelm and anxiety, and the more likely we are to begin a downward cycle.

What else can precedents give you? If nothing else, they will give you consistency in both your behaviour and your decision making. If your behaviour is consistent, your team will feel more certain in working with you. They will understand what your roles are and what theirs are. They will understand the flow of work as it enters the organisation, and which elements of the job need your input and which don't.

This consistency, especially if others around you also have clear roles, makes it much easier to manage people and set expectations and accountabilities. When people don't know what success looks like in their day to day because what is and or isn't their responsibility keeps changing, it's very hard for them to be consistent in their output and extremely difficult for you to manage it.

When you are consistent with the work you do and don't do, and regimented in following the business systems, others will see, take note and mimic this behaviour. This sets a culture of accountability, systems thinking and reduction of key-person risk, all of which are critical in breaking through the entrepreneurial ceiling.

Last but not least, working in an environment where precedent matters will bring certainty to your working world. It's like driving to a destination you haven't been to before. Without Google Maps it can be an anxious trip, full of unknowns and marked by indecision as you second-guess yourself. If you use Google Maps, you don't have to make any decisions. You simply follow the direction the app gives you and calmly make your way to your destination, whether you have been there before or not.

Fear of the unknown and fear of losing what you have are major barriers to shifting behaviours and breaking through the entre-preneurial ceiling. But in this new world, where decisions are made once and then the precedent is set, the unknown becomes known and you will have a wonderful feeling of being in control. This calm and clarity give you the sense of wellbeing, space and clean air that you need to lift your eyes to a different future and start to chase your business by design.

What precedents do you need to set in your day to day? Identify how these will work in the daily workflows for you and your team. If possible, set the rules inside a business system that supports their implementation and guides you and your team members. Involve the team in the new processes and ensure they are clear how it works in their role and what their accountabilities are. Once embedded and operating effectively, go and find a new prec-edent that liberates you from the day to day. Rinse and repeat.

Creating precedents is incredibly liberating. You basically don't have to think. You can align your day-to-day behaviours with your long-term goals using predetermined decisions. In doing so, you can hack your natural evolutionary inclinations without going through the daily struggle that ultimately leads you to give into temptation, customer demands and the path of least resistance.

Align your strategy with your business by design

In his book *Good Strategy Bad Strategy*, Richard Rumelt put it very succinctly when he wrote, 'Any coherent strategy pushes resources towards some ends and away from others.' Applying this thinking to your task of liberating yourself to create your future world, you might as well push organisational resources towards the ends that align with your business by design.

This is great in theory, but how can we make this practical so everyone in the organisation can align with your strategic direction? What does it look like and what aren't we doing any more? These questions are perfectly normal, and the question of how we are going to do this is the natural default of the entrepreneur. However, Rumelt sees things differently.

In looking at a problem and a solution, Rumelt says:

> 'People normally think of strategy in terms of action – a
> strategy is what an organisation does. But strategy also
> embodies an approach to overcoming a difficulty ... To
> gain a change in perspective, shift your attention from
> what is being done to why it is being done. A good strat-
> egy defines a critical challenge. What is more, it builds a
> bridge between that challenge and action.'

Thinking about Rumelt's concept of strategy as a means to overcome difficulty and point organisational resources towards a
specific direction, rather than as a group of actions an organisation does, is a wonderful perspective for you who are trying to
create a different future. This perspective provides an alternative
thinking pattern. Deeply consider alignment between your purpose and your actions – through the simple question of why are
you doing this and how does it truly contribute to achieving your
strategic goal, your business by design? While I touched on this
earlier in terms of preparing for your entrepreneurial journey, I
want you to look at your why in the context of a decision making
enabler that will guide success without your intervention. I have
also spoken previously about the role of strategy in being able,
in the moment, to help you get out of the weeds by providing a
context and perspective that shifts your state from reactive and
overwhelmed to proactive and in control. This is a different, but
just as effective use of strategy. Strategy as a guide.

> *Questioning your daily activities through the lens of your purpose will take you off autopilot and stop you defaulting to doing what you have always done the way you have always done it.*

By asking why and creating the habit and ritual of doing so, you can set yourself, your organisation and your people on a deliberate, predetermined path of your choosing. If executed consistently, this direction by design, rather than by default, should lead to better outcomes. Outcomes aligned with your purpose, your direction, your business by design.

Aligning your business systems with your organisational why, and ensuring the rules and actions in the day to day truly align with your purpose, is critical to stay on the chosen path. To paraphrase an exchange between Lewis Carroll's Alice in Wonderland and the Cheshire Cat, 'If we don't know where we are going any path will do.' This idea resonates with me. Having done the work in understanding your strategic direction, any intervention that allows you to correct and helps you stay the path should be encouraged.

When driving on a multilane highway on a long trip, it is easy to drift off in thought and get distracted. You may find your vehicle drifting out of your lane. Many roads have small raised bumps between the broken white lines, and when your tyre runs over these it makes a loud noise and thumps the suspension of the vehicle. You are jarred from your inattentive state and act to correct your course.

Strategy is like the white lines. It guides you on your path. Just like driving long distances, it's easy to get distracted and drift away on your entrepreneurial journey. You need to have some raised bumps on the road that alert you when you drift off track, and enable you to correct your course and get back to the real question of why you are doing what you're doing.

Many people overthink what these ripple bumps should be. I have three useful interventions that, when applied consistently, provide the jolt that will help you recognise the drift and get you back on course. This is by no means an exhaustive list, but these are simple routines that I have found aid discipline and help entrepreneurial business owners like yourself stay the course.

Data-driven strategic alignment

The first ripple bump I want to suggest is a qualitative and quantitative scoreboard (report) that you review monthly. Set goals that indicate progress in your strategic direction and behaviour that is aligned with the organisational why. Quantitative indicators could include revenue, gross profit, net profit, equity, debtors, working capital, sick days, retention rates or other more specific industry measures. Set a target and create a way of measuring data that informs the scoreboard, and get consistent in reviewing it. Quantitative data could include good behaviour witnessed across the team, customer commentary, work quality, examples of team work, camaraderie and discretionary effort that aligns with your strategic direction. It doesn't really matter what your scorecard measures, as long as those measures are lead indicators of outcomes aligned with achieving your strategic intent – whatever that looks like for you.

The second ripple bump is the identification of operational issues and challenges that are not aligned with your purpose and strategic direction. You need to create a culture that embraces identifying these issues and problems. I'm sure you don't particularly want to hit these ripple bumps as you drive down the road, but if you do, then they may well save your life. Looking at problems and challenges in a similar light enables you to correct course, put appropriate systems and rules in place to prevent the issue from happening again, and continue to evolve your business systems. Having mechanisms to bring issues to light and a system-based solution to resolve them will provide a continuous-improvement environment hungry for feedback and single minded in raising the bar.

The third ripple bump I want to recommend is to get yourself a mentor who makes you accountable and is not afraid to challenge you when they feel you or your organisation has drifted from your lane. A mentor can be internal or external to your organisation. Internal mentors can be applied to multiple layers of the organisation. Leaders in your team can be buddied up with someone both you and they trust. A mentor or buddy program requires clear guidelines and training that sets out the role of both participants and ensures it is a positive, rather than punitive experience for both parties. Always talk to the systems fix, and work hard on supporting individual capability growth and development. Steering clear of blame takes practice and training, but is an incredibly valuable cultural asset to build towards your business by design.

It may be beneficial to have an independent person chair your monthly meetings to provide another level of accountability and consistency. Set your benchmark, measure your data and consistently take action to stay on course. Having a skilled external mentor is a great way to achieve accountability in your business life. They can be the ultimate version of a ripple bump. Without the influence of the operational day to day to worry about, they can often see things more clearly than you.

Aligning your organisational strategy with your why and putting in place ripple bumps enables your organisation to continue to develop. It facilitates a culture that creates momentum through the entrepreneurial ceiling and beyond chaos and overwhelm.

Create a project

Just like the modelling business example, creating a project or projects that don't rely on you, but rather focus on the business systems of the organisation and therefore foster leadership and capability building opportunities for your team, is an easy way to get out of your own way.

Identifying projects is the trick. Start with revisiting your aspiration and the means you have determined to get there. Consider different ways of getting there that you may not have considered. For example, our modelling business had labour constraints and struggled to attract staff to a remote location. They identified a different way of working and looked overseas to resolve what was a regionalised problem. In considering your organisational aspiration, look at a range of different ways of getting there. Cast your net broadly and leave nothing other than the totally absurd off the table. When looking at a problem as a metaphorical wall, consider ways you could go through it, around it, under it or over it.

Next, narrow down your options until you have three. Take a day or two to let these percolate, then make your choice. They must be projects that can be done with minimal input from you. Your role, once begun, will be overseeing and reviewing. Nothing more.

Next, design a brief for your team.

- What are the outcomes we are looking to achieve?
- What resources are available?
- How much time are you able to allocate to your project heads?
- Who is in charge and what are their accountabilities in running the project?

Map bite-size targets broken down into key milestones, along with touch points and reporting mechanisms that keep you informed and confident.

Bring in your team. Launch the project and make it important. Tell the team how the project fits into the broader organisational strategy and aspirations. Let them know why it is important. Build the emotion and get them excited. Game on!

Don't make the mistake of launching and abdicating. Abdicating rather than delegating is where we hand over the project and wipe our hands of it. Stay interested, stay engaged, keep up the momentum. Your job, like a snow plough in winter, is to clear the path and give your team every opportunity to succeed. Finally, ensure that your team has blocks of access to you, especially during the ramp up and launch phase, then, as much as practicable... get out of your way.

> *The problem with entrepreneurs is, as a rule, you're a pretty impatient lot.*

It is mission critical that we allow enough time for our people to grow into the leadership of the project. I often hear business owners say, 'It's so frustrating. How come I can do it and they can't?' Well, the reality is, you don't want your employees to have the same wiring and skill set that you have. If they did, they would probably leave and create a business of their own. Take your time. Be patient, and remember – your role is to support and coach them through, not do.

Remember, also, that there is a long-term game at play here.

Now let's get an update on our modelling business.

When we left our business earlier in this chapter, they had just made the decision to focus on growing their capability locally and withdrawn from the overseas experiment. In early 2021, the business put on five local 'cadets', who were undertaking a gap year after completing Year 12. By the end of 2022, four remained. These four had decided to do further study, but elected to continue working in the business while undertaking distance education through a hybrid work/study model. They grew their capability dramatically in that first year and are progressing through what is now a well-defined career path.

The business itself had its best commercial year, and in July 2021 was involved in an exciting merger with two partner businesses that has made it part of a bigger supply chain. Yes, this business became an attractive prospect that merged with one of the businesses showcased in the previous chapters. The business continues to win projects of significance, which is critical in keeping the people engaged through interesting and purposeful work. It provides the variety they seek in their day to day while continuing to challenge their individual and collective capabilities.

The owner has gone on to become general manager of the merged entity, and seamlessly promoted the highly capable former second in charge as the leader of the modelling business. While business is not always smooth sailing and the nature of a successful business is to solve problems, this business has transitioned successfully to a sustainable and system-driven operation with minimal key-person risk and empowered leadership.

The business today has twenty-five staff who have clear roles and responsibilities, a well-defined career path, crystal-clear understanding of what success looks like in each position and an understanding of how they progress.

The new leader has developed into a skilled communicator and empathetic leader who motivates his people and strives to move the business forward. He is, like his predecessor, a calm, well considered individual who has found a way to get the best out of his people. His proclivity to professional development continues to see him thrive and grow in his new role.

Today's success story is the result of deliberate action taken five years earlier when the entrepreneurial leader decided to find a different way. A direction that set the path and enabled the company to break through the entrepreneurial ceiling, scale the entrepreneurial ladder and create a scalable, visionary and rewarding business.

In building capacity through projects and processes without his direct involvement, the leader was able to create breakthrough infrastructure that did not rely on him. In doing so, he was able to do what many leaders have not – he got out of his own way.

BREAKTHROUGH
BITES

- There are things you can do to get through the entrepreneurial ceiling without having to rely on willpower alone.

- Until you truly decide to follow a different path, the journey through the entrepreneurial ceiling cannot commence.

- Just like a legal precedent, the ability to apply a decision precedent in circumstances where choices and decisions must be made in the day-to-day business is incredibly useful in staying the course.

- The trick is to have a set of rules or precedents prepared, which takes the decision making away in the moment.

- When people don't know what success looks like in their day to day because the goal posts keep moving, it's very hard for them to be consistent in their output and extremely difficult for you to manage it.

- In this new world where decisions are made once and then the precedent is set, the unknown becomes known and you will have a wonderful feeling of being in control.

- The idea that you would question your daily activities through the lens of your purpose is designed to take you off autopilot and defaulting to what you have always done the way you have always done it.

- Aligning organisational strategy with your why and putting in place ripple bumps enables your organisation to continue developing.

- The problem with entrepreneurs is that, as a rule, you are a pretty impatient lot. It is mission critical that we allow enough time for our people to grow into the leadership of the project.

CONCLUSION

Back Yourself

Over to you

If you look back through your life, you will be able to see slid-ing doors moments when you made impactful decisions that sent you down one path and not another. It might have been the decision to leave your job to start or buy your business. It might have been plucking up the courage to ask your partner to marry you. It might have been your first kiss in a new relationship. All these moments, and you will have your own examples, are like a photo, a frozen snapshot in time of the moment your feet left the bungee-diving platform and there was no going back.

I would like you to tap into these moments and try to capture the essence of what it was that inspired you and propelled action. Was it that the vision of what could-be was so crystal clear that nothing else seemed an option? Was it a surge of courage that coursed through your veins at that moment that lit you up and made you brave? Was it simply that the status quo was no longer bearable for you? Whatever it was, I want you to write it down, distil it to its essence and keep it with you at all times.

This will be your superpower. In times of self-doubt, challenge and overwhelm – and there will be many – call on your essence against the backdrop of your inspirational vision and get out of the weeds. Create a new perspective. One which changes your state of being and, like the ripple bumps on the road, realigns you and gets you back in your lane.

In an emergency... break glass!

The journey through the entrepreneurial ceiling will be littered with sliding doors moments. Moments when you make small decisions, such as doing a piece of work yourself rather than delegating, executing a business system work-around because you can and it will bring short-term outcomes, allowing every decision to come through you. In the moment, these may seem small, innocuous actions of little consequence, but they're not. Each of these small decisions will ripple across the organisational pond and create far and wide impacts. They are signs that you're not prepared to stay the new path you have created. You are destined to an organisational life of porpoising below the entrepreneurial ceiling. You are forfeiting a business by design.

In my view, there has never been a better time to be an entrepreneur. Technological platforms that are easy to use and cheap to access have changed the game, and the guys and girls in the garage have never had a more level playing field. The internet has given us, for the first time in history, the ability to access almost all the knowledge we require to be successful. We are living longer, healthier, more affluent lives. So, with all these things going for us, why are so many people trapped below the entrepreneurial ceiling?

This book provides the actions, structures and systems to break through the entrepreneurial ceiling, but you must be the spark. You must walk towards the challenges that confront you, get comfortable with being uncomfortable and summon the internal fortitude to make it happen. There will be elements that will play to your entrepreneurial strengths and will come naturally, such as your proclivity to action, and there will be elements that will be unfamiliar and confronting. Amplify your strengths, mitigate your weaknesses, and do the often-uncomfortable work that is building a business by your design.

Having had the privilege of observing entrepreneurs up close in your natural habitat for over twenty years, I am always inspired by your energy, your creativity and your passion for what you do. I have learned so much from these encounters, and they have been instrumental in shaping who I am today and how I mentor. I have the deepest admiration and respect for what each of you are able to achieve in the day to day and how you have built your businesses. You are amazing!

My greatest wish for you is to create the business you dreamed of when you started this journey. A life of freedom and choice. A life where you don't turn up to a job every day out of necessity, but turn up as the best version of yourself – inspired, passionate, enthusiastic and committed.

My deepest wish for you is that you create your business by design.

Connect with Me

Thank you for reading *Business by Design*.

Hopefully I have provided you with some food for thought in how you run your entrepreneurial business in the day to day, and a glimpse into a different future. A future you design that lives up to the dreams and aspirations you had when you started this adventure.

It would give me great pleasure to see this used as your playbook in building your business by design. A business free of stress, worry and anxiety. A business that provides you with the option to choose and make the choices that serve you and your family.

I would love to connect with you and hear your stories, and hopefully get some tips and tricks that you have discovered in transitioning through the entrepreneurial ceiling. Please feel free to email me. I would love to hear from you!

If you enjoyed this book, you might like to read my twice weekly LinkedIn blog and email newsletter.

Please email businessbydesign@chrisgreen.au if you would like to be on my list.

I have a group coaching and mentor program specifically for entrepreneurial businesses like yours called, appropriately, Business by Design. This provides a wonderful opportunity to work within a structured online peer environment to become confident, in control and connected. Please feel free to go to www.chrisgreen.au to learn more. While you're there, I encourage you to watch the videos of businesses, just like yours, that I have worked with on their journey.

Finally, I run an annual business immersion event. This is an opportunity for likeminded business owners to come together, learn from me and industry leaders, and spend two full days working on your business. Again, please go to my website for upcoming event details.

Acknowledgments

I am incredibly privileged to have had the opportunity to share the journey with so many great leaders, people and families since 2001. Prior to this, in 1996, I learned how challenging running your own family business really is when my wife and I purchased the Everton Hotel. This was situated in the rural village where I grew up. We worked eighteen hours a day, seven days a week. The rest of the time was our own. It was a wonderful introduction to the challenges and plight of you, the entrepreneur.

By my side the whole way has been my wife, Lisa. Always backing me, always supportive, always barracking. It has been an amazing ride and we have done this together. I am incredibly blessed having you as my life partner, and I couldn't have done it without you. My adult kids, Charlotte and Aaron, have also sacrificed a lot. I wasn't always there as I built my practice when they were growing up, but I love being a dad and I did my best. My parents, John and Fran, have been my biggest advocates. They are the ones cheering the loudest from the stands and backing me at every opportunity.

It's fair to say that it is my clients who made this book possible. Most of what I have learned I learned from you. The case studies in this book are based on real-life business owners whom I work with today. They are amazing. They keep showing up day in and day out, determined, resilient and passionate. Your energy and insights never cease to amaze. Your friendship and support of me and my practice has been remarkable, and I am just so grateful.

I would like to note the following businesses, whose stories have featured heavily in this book. Stanton and Killeen Winery, Coons Dairy, RCE Australia, Coolamon Chaser Bins, Net Intellect, Yarrawonga Manufactured Housing, Roddy Engineering, Bright Brewery, Scope PC, Rapid Hydraulics, Larsen Engineering, Pastro Ag, Crighton Engineering, Connex, CPE Construction, CGC Group, Farm Tech, Tallangatta Meat Processors, Grealy Motors, Blue Gum Farm, Morgan Couzens, Burder Industries (Superaxe), Discount Grocery Warehouse, Habitat Planning, Hargreaves Joinery, Longford Civil, John B. Electrical, Ovens and King Builders, Peak Surveyors, Peter Bowen Homes, Streamology, Quantech Design, Roberson Construction, Mitta Dairies, Lecroma, Landmark Harcourts Wangaratta, Riverina Fire Solutions, Annix and Peter Sadler Transport. There is a piece of each of your stories throughout the book, and it is your collective wisdom that inspires me every day. I know I have missed many other businesses that have supported me on my journey, but you know who you are.

To the Wang Maggies Punters and Brunswick Amateur Golfers, you keep me grounded and sane. No ego could survive you lot.

My whole world operates because Amy arranges it so. A huge thank you to Amy Bonnici, who keeps my world spinning from across the ditch in New Zealand. An amazingly organised business manager who, despite the time difference and long hours, continually helps me get better and is the bridge between myself and my clients that we have all come to rely on.

Thank you to the colleagues I have worked with over the years who have taught me my craft. Special thanks to Tony Irish, Mark Schultz, Sonia Petering, Sue Robertson (RDV), Tim Farrar, Vance Wheeler, Emma McQueen, Dermott Crowley, Matt Church and Lisa O'Neill who got me my start in this caper and/or have accelerated my growth.

I truly hope the insights in this book help you in your entrepreneurial endeavours. It is a challenging road you have chosen, and it is my wish that the stories of others and lessons outlined in this book will make your journey just that little bit easier.

Referenced Books

- *Good to Great: Why Some Companies Make the Leap and Others Don't* – Jim Collins
- *Entrepreneurship* – Marc Dollinger
- *Blue Ocean Strategy* – W. Chan Kim and Renee Mauborgne
- *The Barefoot Investor* – Scott Pape
- *Shoe Dog* – Phil Knight
- *Traction* – Gino Wickman
- *Daring Greatly* – Brené Brown
- *Play Fair but Win* – Michael Dell
- *Man's Search for Meaning* – Victor Frankl
- *Grit* – Angela Duckworth
- *Thriving in Complexity* – Alex Hagan
- *Breaking the Habit of Being Yourself* – Dr Joe Dispenza
- *Essentialism, The Disciplined Pursuit of Less* – Greg McKeon
- *The E-Myth Revisited, Why Most Small Businesses Don't Work and What to Do About It* – Michael Gerber
- *Systemology* – David Jenyns
- *Smart Work* – Dermott Crowley
- *How to Lead a Quest* – Dr Jason Fox

- *Leaders Eat Last* – Simon Sinek
- *Concept of the Corporation* – Peter Drucker
- *The Culture Code* – Daniel Coyle
- *Trillion Dollar Coach* – Eric Schmidt
- *Outliers* – Malcolm Gladwell
- *The Upside of Stress* – Dr Kelly McGonigal
- *Atomic Habits* – James Clear
- *Willpower Instinct* – Dr Kelly McGonigal
- *Good Strategy Bad Strategy* – Richard Rumelt

Notes

1. https://www.girlboss.nz/
2. https://www.abs.gov.au/statistics/economy/business-indicators/counts-australian-businesses-including-entries-and-exits/latest-release
3. https://hbr.org/2009/09/how-strategy-shapes-structure
4. https://www.thomasedison.org/inventions
5. https://www.sciencedirect.com/science/article/pii/S0960982211011912
6. https://www.britannica.com/biography/J-P-Morgan
7. https://www.youtube.com/watch?v=TQMbvJNRpLE
8. https://www.sciencedirect.com/science/article/pii/S2213058615300097
9. Downfall The Case Against Boeing – Netflix